# OF CABBAGES AND KINGS

*The History of Allotments*

# OF
# CABBAGES
# AND
# KINGS

*The History of Allotments*

## CAROLINE FOLEY

F

FRANCES LINCOLN LIMITED

PUBLISHERS

*For* Jesse Maurice

Frances Lincoln Limited
74–77 White Lion Street
London N1 9PF
www.franceslincoln.com

First Frances Lincoln edition 2014

A catalogue record for this book is available from the British Library.

Designed by Arianna Osti

978 0 7112 3409 3

Printed and bound in China

1 2 3 4 5 6 7 8 9

# CONTENTS

# PROLOGUE

TAKING A TRAIN from Coventry earlier this year, it struck me that the history of allotments was unfolding backwards before my eyes.

First came the railway plots along the line – the familiar image seen from the train in the suburbs of every industrial city in England and Wales. They are the wartime plots established when the government of the day was cajoling or shaming (whatever it took) the population to take on a plot and get digging. Wartime was allotment heyday. It is said that by 1943 the 1.4 million allotment plots, laid end to end, would have stretched from London to Dumfries.

As my train lumbered into the countryside, a patchwork of fields defined by thick hawthorn hedges covered in May flowers – still so typical of the British landscape – came into view. This is the living evidence of eighteenth- and nineteenth-century 'enclosures', when one-third of the total agricultural land in England was snatched into private hands. One-third of that was the commons.

I wished that the square tower of a Norman church would next appear, to illustrate the beginning. It did not, alas, but then I recalled that allotment people, a stalwart and cussed lot, still talk in terms of 'rods', 'poles' and 'perches'. All three the same measurement, they represent the distance between the back of the plough and the nose of the ox. This surely brings us back to medieval agriculture, practised at the time of William the Conqueror, and so to the very roots of allotments.

Drovers at work.

To wrong another by the name of right;
Thus came enclosure – ruin was its guide,
But freedom's cottage soon was thrust aside
And workhouse prisons raised upon the site.
E'en nature's dwellings far away from men,
The common heath, became the spoiler's prey;
The rabbit had not where to make his den
And labour's only cow was drove away.

John Clare, 'The Fallen Elm' (1820s)

# INTRODUCTION

NOWADAYS, WHEN SOMEONE heads off to their allotment it will be to enjoy a spot of gardening and perhaps compare notes with their fellow plot holders. Quite likely, it will be to take a break from the hectic pace of life and unwind in peace and quiet. It could equally be to spend time among the wildlife flooding into their green oasis. They might come to satisfy a desire to muddy their hands and breathe fresh air after a day spent in a stuffy office or flat. Or, on doctor's orders, to get fit.

Allotmenteers grow vegetables and fruit because home-grown is fresher than they can buy, and probably (but by no means necessarily) cheaper. They can grow unusual and exotic vegetables, or delights that you cannot find in shops because they wilt too quickly for any shelf life. Plot holders can guarantee, if they wish, that their produce will be unpolluted, organic and naturally ripened by the sun. In short, for most people, allotments these days are held for pleasure more than for grinding necessity.

Yet it was not always so. Look back and you will find that allotments had little to do with leisure. Land to grow food was the vital lifeline for poor country people – the serfs, peasants, agricultural workers or 'labouring poor', as they were variously known. For them land and the right to dig could make the difference between independence – however meagre – and the destitution of the workhouse.

The history of allotments touches on wider events and is shaped by forces that may seem unconnected to today's allotment gardener. It is a story of greed and power, of hunger, protest and the struggle

Peasants drinking.

for a fairer society. It concerns the arrogance of the ruling and rising middle classes and their indifference to the plight of the poor – but also philanthropy, the pursuit of ideals and, eventually, some beneficent legislation.

So, why does the past matter to us? Perhaps it is a call to keep in mind that dangers still lurk, that we should not take our plots for granted. It certainly provides a further perspective on how fortunate we are to have access to peaceful havens where we can grow food cheaply. History also provides a poignant reminder of the fact that if an allotment plot is today more or less a citizen's right – despite the long waiting lists – this is largely due to past generations fighting tooth and nail for land. We owe them at least a nod of appreciation.

The battle for land has been an unequal one throughout history. On the one side is profit and, on the other, the most unprofitable needs of the poor. It seems something of a miracle that in the end altruism won over the aims and ambitions of the powerful – even if spurred on by less-than noble fears of revolution, and later, in the twentieth century, by fears of defeat at war. But the battle is not over. Despite the fact that 'statutory' allotments, the vast majority, are protected by law to a great extent, we cannot afford to be complacent. Other priorities, like housing, continue to compete for space with the 300,000 plots currently occupying 18,210 hectares (45,000 acres) in England and Wales.

The precedent for allotments goes back beyond historical records. In customs formalized under the law of medieval manor courts, the peasant had use of a piece of the common land, or the 'commons', so he could grow his own food, at very least for subsistence. By 'common right' he could also graze livestock and collect fuel. History relates how he was cheated of this born right and how, eventually, he got it back in a smaller measure in the form of allotments.

The Liberal statesman David Lloyd George, speaking in 1913, more than 800 years after the Norman Conquest, regretted that the right to land had been 'stolen' from the medieval peasant, bringing hardship and humiliation over the centuries that followed:

'He had his common where he could graze a cow that would give him milk and butter for his children. There was a little patch where he could grow corn to feed them. There he had his poultry, his geese, his pigs; a patch of land where he could grow green produce for his table. He was a gentleman; he was independent. He had a stake in his country. His title was as ancient and apparently indefensible as that of the lord of the manor.'

So, to get a true perspective on the history of allotments we need to start with their foundation stone – the common land. The first chapter describes the daily round of the serf, his entitlement to the commons and his place in the village in a simple farming society.

The feudal system began to crumble when the Black Death decimated the population in the 1300s. The war-mongering medieval kings imposed massive poll taxes to finance their fruitless wars with France. The peasants were pinned down to their villages, with their wages capped.

The sixteenth century saw the end of serfdom. However, it liberated not just the serf from the master, but also the master from the serf. The lords of the manor seized the opportunity to switch to the more profitable and less work-intensive business of sheep farming. Many of the arable lands that had kept agricultural workers occupied throughout the year were converted to pasture.

The landowners – including the now rising class of yeomen – began to cast a covetous eye on the large acreage of the peasants' common land. They came to private agreements on enclosing it and sharing it out among themselves. Quite often they broke the common law in the comfortable knowledge that the consequences would not be too harsh.

With nothing now to their names but their labour for hire, many peasants fell into pauperism. As beggars and 'rogues forlorn', they became a serious headache to the state. The Elizabethan poor laws followed and the first workhouses were built in an early shot at welfare provision. This was the start of a series of poor laws, none of which attempted more than to keep body and soul together, until the welfare state was introduced in the twentieth century.

Though enclosures were gathering momentum from the seventeenth century onwards, it was between 1750 and 1850 that agricultural Britain was changed from wide open countryside to the series of small fenced fields so familiar today. Around 2 million hectares/5 million acres (one-third of farmland) were enclosed by private parliamentary acts. Whole villages were swept away, along with the community life of centuries. True, there was the need to maximize agriculture to feed a burgeoning population – but the needs of the peasants were barely considered.

Decommissioned soldiers and sailors returning from the Napoleonic Wars, along with the Irish poor, further flooded the labour market in the early nineteenth century. Agricultural machinery began to replace manual labour. Particularly resented were the threshing machines that took away the main source of employment in winter.

Without access to land, farm labourers had lost their buffer against hard times and high food prices. Still largely illiterate, they were not in a position to argue their case. They rioted instead. This had little effect in the lofty chambers of Westminster. The riots were brutally quashed, ending in mass transportation and hangings.

Into this tragic scenario stepped a few heroes. Arthur Young, who in 1793 became secretary to the newly formed Board of Agriculture, was possibly the first person of influence to sue for allotments. In his travels around Britain he had observed that having some land gave the labourers self-respect and the incentive to work.

In the late 1820s, the fearless and eloquent William Cobbett stalked the farmers at their meetings, giving his 'Rustic Harangues' to persuade, or shame them into making a 'countryman's alliance' with labourers and smaller tenant farmers, to promote their mutual interests in Parliament.

The late eighteenth century saw the first Allotment Movement, pioneered by the Society for Bettering the Condition and Increasing the Comforts of the Poor. The first 'allotments' of land, either attached to a cottage or in the form of fields shared out in sizeable plots of up to 0.6 hectares/1.5 acres per family, were largely used for growing wheat. However, it was Benjamin Wills, a London surgeon, who really put the Allotment Movement into top gear when he founded the Labourers' Friend Society in 1831, with an influential membership of concerned gentry, bishops and politicians. Debate followed in the highest circles on the best form of land provision. Should it be potato grounds, cow pastures, 'a cow and a cott', smallholdings, land attached to cottages, or allotments? An important motivation in providing land was to improve the workers' morals and to keep them out of the alehouse.

In the 1870s another landmark was reached when Joseph Arch, a hedge-cutter by trade, set up a labourers' union, became an MP and worked on the Third Reform Act of 1884, which gave the working man some voice. In 1886 Jesse Collings, a Birmingham-born travelling salesman, brought Lord Salisbury's government down over the allotment question, and worked tirelessly at his crusade for land reform under the banner of 'Three Acres and a Cow'.

As this book encompasses a broad swathe of history, I have taken great strides through the centuries, only pausing now and then to set the next scene. The facts and figures owe everything to historians, ancient, old and new – indeed, they are the gentry and I the peasant. It has been a fascinating journey. One thing that stands out for me, as has been remarked before in other contexts, is how often history repeats itself. Many of the historical problems described in these pages are still resounding and remain unsolved today.

One hope I have is to challenge the commonly held belief that allotments sprung from the Dig for Victory campaign during the Second World War, when the public at large was urged to cultivate allotments and grow produce in every inch of space as a patriotic duty to help to feed the nation.

In fact, the twentieth-century wartime allotments represent a complete about-turn in their long, turbulent history. Although in the mid-nineteenth century the parishes began to provide allotments, the main source was still the private landowner, mostly the gentry. It was not until 1908 and the Small Holdings and Allotment Acts that local authorities were bidden to provide them. And it was not until 1919 – when the British population had striven to feed itself and the number of plots had risen to 1.5 million – that the definition of allotments as destined for the 'labouring population' was struck off the statute books and allotments were officially open to all.

My aim in this book is to explain how allotments came about as the largely begrudging response to the misery of the poorest people in the country. Like many valuable things, they were immensely hard to gain but would be so easy to lose – irrevocably.

# 1. THE SERF & THE COMMONS 1066–1349

'It is the custom in England,
as in other countries, for the nobility
to have great power over the common
people, who are their serfs.'

*Froissart's Chronicles* (1395)

Medieval Britain lay under a vast canopy of trees – predominantly oaks and ash on the clay downs, with beech on the limestone of the hills. Gradually, though, the virgin forest was being cleared by fire and axe. In the clearings, there were hamlets or small crudely built villages, mostly with fewer than one hundred inhabitants, sometimes only fifty. Depending on the terrain, there were fields for pasture and areas of common land, where the villagers had their plots. On the plains, these 'commons', as they were known, stretched as far as the eye could see from the small nuclear village. They were divided into seemingly random strips and resembled an allotment site on a giant scale.

The commons of the medieval landscape were the precedent for the allotments provided centuries later. They were an accepted right at a time when society was deeply agrarian and all looked to Mother Earth for sustenance in one way or another. A plot on which to grow food was a crucial part of life for the peasant. It could make the difference between life and death, and was safeguarded by the custom of centuries.

Although land for the peasants is known to have preceded written records, the arrival of William the Conqueror in British history marks a good starting point to this story. Despite his reputation as a tyrant,

William I was an able administrator. He introduced a formal structure to society, where everyone, from the highest to the lowest, had their own secure place and clearly defined rights, enshrined in the law of the manor courts.

William the Conqueror introduced manorialism, in which all, even the most humble serf, had a share in the land.

## The Norman Conquest & the manor

After his 1066 victory in the Battle of Hastings, William, with his archers and crack horsemen, swept through England, taking ownership of the Anglo-Saxon estates. King Harold's troops, fighting on foot, had been no match for the Normans, whose warhorses were percheron stallions. Their cavalrymen rode with spurs for speed and had stirrups – the latest novelty – to help steady their aim. Battleaxes, stones and a few bows and arrows were easily defeated by spear, lance and sword. The south of the country crumbled quickly. The north, which was under the Danelaw, made the mistake of holding out. William's

**Harrying of the North**

swift and terrible vengeance in 1069 became known as the Harrying of the North. Villages were razed and populations massacred between York and Durham. Of those who escaped slaughter, many starved or gave themselves up as slaves.

William swore at his coronation that he would keep the existing laws. At the same time, he introduced manorialism, the feudal system widely practised across Europe in which the king, divinely appointed, owned all the land himself. William, having confiscated the estates of the 'traitor thegns' of the old regime, distributed them to his friends among the Norman aristocracy. They in turn divided up their land further and offered tenancies to the Norman knights who had distinguished themselves in battle and proved their loyalty to the king. The barons and knights, in return for holding land, would raise armies, fight wars and put down rebellions. They built motte-and-bailey castles for defence and as symbols of power. William built the Tower of London as his personal city fortress.

The nobles were handed out several manors in different parts of the country. In this way, and as they were often abroad fighting, it was ensured that none could be on all their estates at one time and become too powerful. While away, they entrusted the management of the manors to the sheriffs. These were French-speaking men of baronial rank who could if necessary be removed by the king. William's aim was *nulle terre sans seigneur* – no land without its lord.

The manor was the unit of land at the heart of the feudal system, usually consisting of a lord's demesne and lands rented to tenants. However, manors varied in structure. In the Midlands the land usually centred on the nucleated village, where houses, church and a single manor were clustered together. In Norfolk it was not unusual to find four manors to one village, whereas in the west of England there might be one manor for four villages and possibly a town. In some areas the uncultivated 'wastes' were so huge that they were shared by many manors and had no known boundaries. The 24,000 hectares/60,000 acres of the New Forest were shared by twenty-one villages. The main grain-growing areas were the lowlands of Yorkshire, Lancashire, Cambridgeshire, the Midlands and the central-south areas of England. These were farmed largely as 'champion land', with big open fields stretching for hundreds of acres.

**Feudal hierarchy** The manorial system was at is most powerful between the middle of the twelfth and fourteenth centuries. The hierarchy of the feudal manor consisted of king, the Norman nobility, knights, and the clergy. William had replaced all key posts in the

Church, which included the archbishops, bishops and abbots, with his own appointments. He Latinized the liturgy and, indebted to the Pope for sanctioning his Holy War against England, gave the Church a fifth of the land in England. One result of this was an architectural renaissance and the building of many churches and monasteries in the Romanesque style.

The peasants, 85 per cent of the population, were on the lowest rung of society. Most worked on the lord's demesne, the manorial land reserved for his own use. Among the peasantry was a further hierarchy. The freemen, yeomen and husbandmen were, often enough, independent smallholders. They paid rent for the land but had few obligations to the lord apart from jury service at the manor courts, overseeing the workers at harvest time and loaning their draft animals, farm equipment or carts as needed. Below them, the serfs and slaves had little or no freedom. They were part of the lord's chattels and therefore could be bought and sold. They were obliged to work for him and commit their heirs to serfdom. The lords, for their part, undertook to protect their serfs from marauders, to provide justice and some land for their subsistence.

**Villeins & serfs**

A medieval monk brewing ale. The Church had huge influence, while the clergy dominated feudal society and demanded tithes.

The largest category of serfs were the villeins. Among them were skilled workers – ploughmen, carters, blacksmiths, basket weavers, carpenters, bakers, shepherds, ironmongers, beekeepers, millers, swineherds and the like. Then came the unskilled bordar or cottar, the cottager. He might only have just enough land to feed his family, so had to pay his dues in extra labour for the lord. Lowest of all was the slave. He owned nothing but 'his belly' and was dependent on handouts from the landlord in return for his service. The 'unfree' peasants were not allowed to leave the estate without permission. Some may have absconded, since the law stated that an escapee who remained undiscovered for a year and a day could claim to be a freeman. However, it was dangerous to strike out for independence. Vagrancy was considered a crime and was severely punished.

According to the Domesday Book of 1086, the peasant population was made up of 12 per cent freemen, 35 per cent villeins, 30 per cent cottagers and 9 per cent slaves. It also recorded the resources of each and every shire in minute detail, so none might escape the king's taxes. An Anglo-Saxon chronicler remarked of King William: 'So narrowly did he cause the survey to be made, that there was not one single hide nor rood of land, nor – it is shameful to tell but he thought it no shame to do – was there an ox, cow or swine that was not set down in the writ.'

The serf paid rent for his strips on the common land in labour, kind or coin – for example, by handing over a proportion of his harvest. Arrangements varied on different manors and according to the size of the serf's shares in the land, and payment could involve a mixture of elements. There was a further fee, known as a merchet, when his daughters married, and a heavier one if he wanted to

In August or September the whole family was pressed into 'boon works'. The wheat was chopped down with a sickle or reap hook. This picture is taken from the 1540 Book of Hours.

send a son to school or to a priest to get some education. When a peasant died, the lord was entitled to his first beast and the Church took second pick as a heriot, or mortuary tax. Livestock, precious to the peasants, was often used to provide dowries and bequests. A share was expected for the lord of the manor when a farm animal was sold. If a peasant wanted to keep poultry, a hen or eggs were required as payment. Rents paid in kind as food were usually payable in the form of chickens at Christmas, eggs at Easter and grain at Martinmas on 11 November. Peasants were obliged to use the master's mill, and both pay and give him a multure, a proportion of the flour.

Further payment was due for the peasant's pigs to root for acorns in the forests, and there was a fine if his beasts strayed. By contrast, the lord's bulls, rams and wild boar could wander freely, helping themselves to crops and mates. The lord had *jus faldae* – the right to fold all the manorial sheep on his own land so the manure would enrich the soil of his fields. The 'tallage at will' was a tax that could be imposed by the lord at whim. In the twelfth century this was modified, so that the amount and frequency were controlled by the 'custom of the manor'.

In addition to the heavy set of dues and services owed to the lord, the serfs were obliged to work free of charge for the **Church tithes** Church and pay tithes, a tax of one-tenth of annual earnings or produce, right down to their vegetables and goose feathers. The tithes were locked up in the hated tithe barns. Along with the magnificent priories and abbeys, these buildings demonstrated the power and wealth of the Church Militant. There were also Mass pennies to be found for the parish church, which serfs would attend on Sundays, Saints' Days (when spared from work), at Christmas, Easter, and for baptisms, marriages and funerals. Wandering friars, pilgrims and wayside crosses in every village were potent daily reminders of Heaven and Hell. Most parish churches had attached to them glebe land, otherwise known as 'church's furlongs' or 'parson's closes'; this was provided as a source of income for the clergy, who would be competing with the peasants at market.

Chaucer's priest was an exception to the general rule. Unusually, he was a villein himself, a shepherd and 'holy man of good renown' who was reluctant to collect the tithes.

> He did not set his benefice to hire
> And leave his sheep encumbered in the mire,
> Or run to London to earn easy bread
> By singing masses for the wealthy dead,
> Or find some brotherhood and get enrolled.
> He stayed at home and watched over his fold.

**A serf's life**  The cottager's house was typically timber-framed, built on a cruck structure in which two upturned V-shaped trees, usually oak, were secured at the top to a ridge pole. The roofs would be thatched with straw or rushes, and the wattle walls pierced with a hole for a window. Mud floors would be covered with straw. At night the farm animals would be brought in to protect them from theft, bears and wolves. Smoke from the fire would escape through a hole in the roof.

Bread and a potage of beans and grain was the peasant's staple diet. Whereas their masters ate refined white bread, the peasants ate a coarser type made of mixed wheat and rye, or maslin. In areas where wheat was not grown, bread was made from oats instead. When times were hard, flour would be made out of peas and beans, an important crop for winter stores; or, when truly desperate, from acorns. Paupers and cottagers were usually permitted to scavenge through the pea and bean fields after harvest, to collect any seeds overlooked. Drinking water was often contaminated as slops went into the same source. The peasants, including children, mostly drank weak beer, or 'small ale', brewed at home.

**The Great Famine**  In 1315–1317 the Great Famine struck, followed by further devastating famines in 1321, 1351 and 1369. Many died of starvation. The lack of food was caused by cold, rainy summers when there was not enough sunshine to ripen corn or process salt by evaporation. The scarcity of salt, a precious commodity, meant that bacon could not be preserved for winter. Sometimes the peasants were forced to eat their most valued possession, their farm animals (also cats, dogs, and even dove dung). As the poor man in William Langland's *Piers Plowman* remarks, there was 'many a wintertime when they suffered much hunger and woe'.

Unlawful gleaning and poaching were common. Nuts, berries, brushwood and furze (gorse) were gathered by women and children from the hedgerows. An illicit kill was often dealt with in the forest and brought back in small pieces to avoid detection. Those caught would generally suffer only a fine – sometimes low enough to be worth the risk. However, should anyone be caught poaching in the royal forests, terrible punishment would ensue under the Norman's harsh 'forest law'. An Anglo-Saxon chronicler records that King William 'made large forests for deer and enacted laws therewith, so that whoever killed a hart or a hind should be blinded'.

An upturned barrel serves as a makeshift table for this outdoor meal. The peasant's staple diet was supplemented by foraging in hedgerows and – more riskily – by poaching.

### The courts

All but the most serious complaints and disputes were settled in the manor court, presided over by the lord or one of his senior officials. The law decreed that the court must be held on manor land, and custom determined the site. Often it was under an oak tree, or in bad weather, in the manor house. It was customary to have a jury of twelve, usually freemen from the estate, and the serfs were bound to attend also. Peasants could go to court with complaints, although they had to pay for the privilege, and hear the 'doom', or opinion, of their fellows, before the judgment of the lord was pronounced.

Murder, rape and breach of the peace, along with criminal charges regarding Crown property, fell to the king's courts. The death sentence was also essentially a royal prerogative, although the manor courts could hang a thief providing he or she was caught red-handed, prosecuted by the loser of the goods, and sentenced and executed in the presence of a royal coroner. There were several coroners in each area to keep an eye on the king's affairs.

## The commons

Over the years, the customs of the manor developed and became hardened into law. In the same way, ancient customs dictated how the land was distributed and farmed. The champion fields were worked on the open-field system. Unfenced, they extended away from the village for hundreds of acres and were divided into a patchwork of strips of up to 0.4 hectares/1 acre each, marked out with stones, sticks or grass-topped ridges (balks). Peasants did not have their strips in a single block, but by custom would have them scattered, uneconomically, around the fields. The lord's demesne might be separate from the village fields or might include strips on the common land. In appearance the open-field system was like a gigantic allotment site stretching as far as the eye could see.

**Virgates**       The largest holdings of strips were measured as 'virgates' or 'yardlands', an area of some 12 hectares/30 acres calculated to be the amount of land a team of two oxen could plough in a season. A wealthy peasant would be a virgator and would be able to run a small market business. Half-virgators could support their family at least. The cottagers, who only had a small croft attached to their dwelling and a few acres besides, would have to do more work for the manor to make ends meet. Stealing the edge of a neighbour's strip was a common offence, as the fights recorded by the manor courts reveal. In *Piers Plowman*, the peasant confesses: 'If I went to the plough I pinched so narrowly that I could steal a foot of land or a furrow, or gnaw the half acre of my neighbour.'

The choice of crops was limited to corn and vetches: wheat, barley or oats for one field, and peas or beans for another. The decision as to which crops would be planted for a particular year would be taken by the 'common assent' of the village in the manor courts. Everyone sowed the same crop. The work would be done by plough teams using pooled oxen. Ploughs were traditionally drawn by a team of eight oxen or horses. Medieval farmers knew about crop rotation and left a third field fallow to regain fertility before being sown the following year, although in some places they kept to a two-field system. After harvest, the peasants could pasture their animals on the open fields, accompanied by herders.

Alongside the commons were the meadows – the only source of hay for feeding animals through winter and for this reason highly valued. They were fenced or ditched and watched over by the hayward. They were called 'lot meadows', as lots were jealously drawn for them. They were also known as 'Lammas lands' because after the hay had been cut, no later than Lammas Day on 1 August, they were open for the village to use for grazing. By-laws restricted grazing rights to the more prosperous commoners who could sustain their animals through winter. This was calculated by the number of acres on the commons that the peasants had at their disposal, as a measure of wealth and as proof that they could provide for the 'levancy' and 'couchancy' – or numbers of days and nights – and afford to keep the animals fed. Areas of uncultivated wasteland or virgin woodlands surrounding the commons and meadows were also used for grazing, and pieces of this land could be rented by the peasants as assarts (from the old French *essarter* – to bring land into cultivation after grubbing up trees).

**Grazing rights**

On the Sunday before Ascension, forty days after Easter, the boundaries of the whole estate were checked at the 'beating of the bounds'. Young and old, led by a parish priest and church officials, would walk the boundaries, offering prayers. The priest would stop at key points, often by an oak, and pray for a good harvest. It was important that the younger generation knew exactly where the boundaries lay, so that this essential information could be preserved for posterity.

In general, the peasants divided their time between their own strips and the lord's. During intense periods of 'boon works', at harvest and other key times in the farming year, they

**Boon works**

might even have to abandon their own crops and the whole family was expected to pitch in for the lord from dawn to dusk. The end of harvest was an occasion for celebration, and the lord of the manor would customarily provide a meal for the peasants, with ale and meat. During the rest of the year, the labour owed to the lord fell into the category of 'week works'.

The peasant's life was measured in a continual round of seasonal tasks. Early in the year, they would spread the straw from the previous season in cowsheds and stables. Marl pits would be dug for their chalky clay to sweeten the soil. The manure from dungheaps by the cottages would be carried back to the fields and ploughed in. Grain was sown from a hopper or 'seed lip' tied round the waist. Peas and beans would be sown individually with a dibber, usually by the women. Next came the time for harrowing, weeding and scaring birds, all essential work if there was to be an abundant harvest. There were ditches to be dug, hedges and enclosures to be repaired, and ploughing to be done. Thistles were dug up after St John's Day on 24 June, as it was believed they would multiply threefold if removed before this date. In late summer the hay was cut with scythes. The fallow ground would get a 'second stirring' to plough in the weeds.

August or September was harvest time and the whole family was pressed into work. The barley, rye, oats, peas and beans were cut with scythes, while the wheat was chopped down with a sickle or reap hook. The ear was cut high up the stalk and the straw was left standing. The sheaves were small enough to be lifted easily. The band for tying them was cut to the length of a man's leg from knee to the sole of the foot. As soon as the corn was cut, the church selected its tithe.

After harvest, the arable land was ploughed and left rough so that winter weather would break down the clods; but land that was to be autumn-sown with wheat or rye would instead be harrowed to a fine tilth. Barley, oats, peas and beans would be sown from February onwards. Post-harvest work also included collecting turves for fires, bracken for cattle bedding and sedge for thatching. Stubble from the cornfields was gathered for use as either thatching or bedding. Any straw that was not needed was ploughed back into the soil.

Women worked as hard as men, on the fields, in the kitchen garden, at brewing and spinning. Bearing and bringing up children was vital to the economy of the household. Many died in childbirth.

Threshing with the flail was standard winter work for the men. The flail was made from two pieces of wood, often thorn, attached together with a leather thong. The thresher would bring down the flail in a rhythmic circular movement to dislodge the grains of corn, which would then be separated from the chaff either by winnowing it with a fan or by tossing it up in the draught of air near a door.

**Threshing & women's work**

The women worked as hard as the men. They helped them on the fields by goading the oxen on, hoeing, weeding, turning hay, tying sheaves, gleaning leftover grain and sowing peas and beans by hand. But their main work was at home, and in the kitchen garden comprising the 'toft', a yard around the house, and piece of land, or 'croft', next to it. A survey carried out in Norfolk found traces of elderberry, sloe, poppy, hemp, linseed, celery, raspberry, strawberry, cherry, apple, plum, bullace and medlar on the site of an eleventh-century croft.

Women also looked after the fire, cooked, took care of the chickens, the geese and the pig. They brewed, or made butter and cheese, and went to market to sell their produce. They pulled hemp and flax up by the roots for thread, rope or linen. The plants were dried, put in the river to soften, cleaned by beating and hung up in 'strikes' before being separated out and spun into yarn. Hemp would be used for candlewicks, shoelaces, halters, girths and bridles.

In winter, while the men repaired their tools, fashioned mugs out of bone and carved beechen bowls and spoons, the women plaited straw of reed for neck collars, stitched and stuffed sheepskin bags for cart saddles, and made candles. Nearly all peasant women were 'spinsters', so much so that the spinning wheel came to symbolize the woman's sphere of work – as illustrated by the medieval poem 'The False Fox':

> The good-wyfe came out in her smok,
> And at the fox she threw her rok [spindle].
> The good-man came out with his flayle,
> And smote the fox upon the tayle.
> *Anon.*

Bearing and bringing up children was vital for the economy of the household. Infant mortality was high, with a death rate of some 30– 50 per cent in the first few days after birth alone. Taking this into account, the average life expectancy was only thirty-one years. Many women died in childbirth. During the childbearing years, their life expectancy was half that of men.

## Medieval enclosures

Magna
Carta
1215

The Magna Carta, signed under duress by King John in 1215, laid the foundation stone for a state governed by civil rights and the rule of law. A key clause was that 'No freeman shall be arrested or imprisoned … except by the lawful judgment of his peers or by the law of the land.' Let it be noted that the Great Charter excluded the 'unfree'. Under the feudal system, wealth had accumulated despite the foolish extravagance of William the Conqueror's successors. More land was brought into cultivation. Flocks and herds flourished and multiplied, even with losses due to the animal diseases collectively known 'murrain'. The population of England, which stood at 1.5 million at the time of the Domesday Book in 1086, had at least doubled by the fourteenth century, despite the famines of 1315–1317 and recurrent bouts of the pestilence.

With the need to provide for a growing population, there was pressure on land. The Statute of Merton of 1235, brought in during the reign of Henry III, John's son, was England's **Statute of Merton** first piece of enclosure legislation. This law confirmed accepted practice by permitting enclosures on common land, but stipulated that enough land should be left to satisfy tenants' rights to have 'free access to the common'. The earliest enclosures (originally 'inclosures') were mostly uncontested and undocumented private arrangements. A hedge or other barrier was put around land, usually common land, which thus became private property. The land was said to be held in 'severalty', reserved for the sole use of the owner or their tenants, and common rights were removed. Local reactions to enclosure varied depending on the quality of the agricultural land. In Kent, Essex and Devon, where there was plenty of pasture, amicable agreements were generally reached with the open-field farmers to a rearrangement of the strips and the annexing of part of the land into private hands for pasture. Where pasture was in short supply, proposals to enclose would have met fierce resistance as the right to graze their animals on the stubble of the cornfields was jealously safeguarded by the peasants.

In 1349 the status quo was severely shaken when disaster struck in the form of the Black Death. In Europe it killed one in three people. All knew, without the smallest doubt, that this was God's vengeance for their sins and that the world was coming to an end. Life did go on, but it was the beginning of the end for feudalism, village life on the manor and farming on the commons.

# 2. BLACK DEATH, POLL TAXES & THE PEASANTS' REVOLT

'From the beginning, all men by nature
were created alike, and our bondage
or servitude came in by the most
unjust oppression of naughty men.'
*John Ball*, June 1381

In the centuries that followed the Norman Conquest, feudalism was undermined by a series of dramatic events as well as the gradual effects of social and economic change. The Black Death, in which a third to a half of the known world's population perished, smote Britain in 1348. The death toll was such that labour, once so plentiful, could no longer be taken for granted. For a while, the peasant had a little bargaining power with his masters – although this turned out to be short-lived.

Claims by Edward III (1312–1377) to the French throne led to endless forays and wars with France that Britain could ill afford. Outrageously high poll taxes, three in four years, exacted by low bullying methods from the poorest as much as from the rich, were imposed to raise money for the power-seeking, war-mongering kings.

In 1381, public fury and indignation boiled over in the Peasants' Revolt. Extraordinary to tell, this albeit bloody revolt was so highly organized, single-minded and coordinated that it all but brought down the government in the space of a few weeks. It was to witness the most dramatic confrontation between commoner and king in the whole of British history. The demands of the rebel leaders – notably folk heroes Wat Tyler and John Ball – included a reversal of laws concerning harsh labour conditions enforced since the Black Death and freedom for the serfs. Even though the Peasants' Revolt was

Plague victims suffered with painful boils that could swell up to the size of an apple. Death generally followed within five days.

viciously crushed, it undoubtedly contributed to the slow demise of feudalism, of the commons and the old laws. It was the first of many rural revolts that would play a part in the eventual establishment of allotments.

## The Black Death

The Black Death made its first appearance in central Asia in the early 1330s, then erupted in China. From there, the disease travelled

**Silk routes**

with the great caravans along the medieval trade routes. By 1336 it was in the Crimea, where it is said to have left 85,000 dead. The following year it reached Cyprus and Constantinople. In Alexandria 1,000 people were dying every day, and as many as 7,000 in Cairo.

A Genoese fleet returning from the Black Sea in 1347 was blown off course and arrived in Sicily with a crew of dying sailors. A few days later, when the panic-stricken inhabitants realized the scale of the impending horror, the fleet was driven away ferociously with arrows and war machines – but too late. The plague was swift and deadly. The poet Giovanni Boccaccio, writing later from a pestilent Florence, observed that the Black Death worked so fast that victims 'ate lunch with their friends and dinner with their ancestors in paradise'.

The Black Death affected all levels of society, rich and poor alike. Victims were shunned by friends, family, even the parish priest.

**Most terrible of all the terrors**

The Black Death moved on remorselessly to Marseilles and then to Paris, arriving there in the spring of 1348. It would finish its deathly tour in Norway and Russia, after reaching England by September 1348. The chronicler Geoffrey le Baker of Swinbrook described the arrival of this much-feared disease: 'The seventh year after it began, it came to England and first began in the towns and ports adjoining the seacoasts, in Dorsetshire, where, as in other counties, it made the country quite void of inhabitants so that there were almost none left alive.'

It is now known that the Black Death was probably a combination of three types of plague – bubonic, septicaemic and pneumonic – all caused by the bacterium *Yersinia pestis*. The bubonic form of plague is spread by fleas parasitic on small rodents, typically the black rat. However, the medieval doctors and scientists knew nothing of this. Powerless in the face of the epidemic, they thought that the atmosphere had been poisoned with a 'miasmic' cloud. They looked to Galen, the ancient Greek physician whose works had been transcribed by monks in the twelfth century. He had preached that infection came from

The plague doctor's beak-like mask held aromatics. Bad smells were thought to cause disease.

breathing in putrid gases such as you would find around rotting corpses, or in stagnant marshes and ponds. To protect themselves from the terrible smell associated with the disease, people burned juniper, laurel, pine, beech, rosemary, camphor and sulphur. Robert of Avesbury, chronicler at the court of Canterbury, observed that the plague 'showed favour to no one, except a very few of the wealthy'. Church bells were rung loudly to drive the plague away. But the only effective course of defence was escape. The wealthy took flight, leaving the poor to fend for themselves in crowded villages.

The peasants became sceptical when they saw that their doctors stood by helplessly, and that the clergy were equally vulnerable and not protected by God any more than they were. The Lincoln chronicler wrote: 'This plague slew Jew, Christian and Saracen alike; it carried off confessor and penitent together. In many places not even a fifth part of the people were left alive. It filled the whole world with terror. Such a great epidemic has never been seen nor heard of before this time.'

It is estimated that 25 million people perished worldwide. In

Western Europe, approximately one-third to half of the population was wiped out in less than three years. In England that represented around 1.5 million people. With fewer hands to work the land, farms were left in a state of neglect and the untilled fields became covered with weeds. Sheep and cattle were left to run wild, rotting in the hedgerows and fields where they died. The death toll left many villages deserted and around 1,000 disappeared off the map completely. Many of those peasants who had survived the Black Death died of starvation in the food shortages that followed.

Others saw their main chance. One consequence of the reduction in England's population from 4 to 2.5 million was to double the market value of labour. The freemen profited by demanding higher wages. The villeins, on the other hand, frustrated that they did not also have the right to work for the highest bidder, chafed at their servitude. As the countryside was in chaos, some serfs slipped away unnoticed to get work from needy landlords in more prosperous parts of the country, no questions asked. Attempts to drag absconders back proved fruitless.

In the first year after the plague, landowners had done well on the much-resented heriots, or mortuary taxes, that serfs were obliged to pay for their dead relatives. But they soon faced serious difficulties, having to pay higher wages while the price of agricultural produce fell steeply, due to lack of demand. The value of farm animals dropped by nearly half. Manufactured goods, on the other hand, which the landlord had to buy, were more expensive because of the dearth of skilled artisans among the surviving population.

**The state of the land**    Following the Black Death much land became free. Grass grew over the strips, blurring the boundaries that defined each labourer's allocation of common land. Any strips left by plague victims who had no heirs could be purloined by the surviving. In this way many peasants had access to more land than before – land that could be made into a more cohesive block than the old system of scattered strips. For the first time, the peasants had a little more land to support themselves and some bargaining power – but not for long. In 1349, Edward III's Ordinance of Labourers, swiftly followed by the Statute of Labourers in 1351, capped their wages to the lowest pre-plague levels of the previous decade. With the limit set at 2d or 3d a day, all hopes of better prospects were effectively dashed.

It was also ordained that every able-bodied person under sixty who had not enough to live on must accept whatever work was offered, or go to prison. Their lords had first call on their labour. The king justified this harsh law by saying that since many of the workers and servants had died in the pestilence, those remaining and seeing 'the straights of the masters ... are not willing to serve unless they receive excessive wages'. Others 'rather than through labour to gain their living, prefer to beg in idleness'.

The peasantry had lost heart and acquired a poor reputation. John Gower, the courtly poet and friend of Chaucer, wrote: 'They are sluggish, they are scarce, and they are grasping. For the very little they do they demand the highest pay.' Some 700 justices were employed to enforce the new legislation. Stocks were set up in every town. Punishment for employers who attempted to raise wages was a 'quarter of a year' prison sentence, doubling in length with every repeat offence thereafter. Branding with the letter 'F' for 'falsity' on the forehead was recommended as a further punishment for law-breakers. Sheriffs were given increased powers to arrest 'evil-doers, rioters and barrators [swindlers]'. In spite of all these measures, the statute proved virtually impossible to enforce because the law of supply and demand was stronger: desperate landowners paid higher wages regardless.

## Poll taxes & the war with France

The king faced other grave problems due to the death toll of the plague. Tax revenue had dropped by one-third, and yet the government had to finance military action against France (in what became known as the Hundred Years War), as well as the continuing battle with France's ally, Scotland. When, in 1377, the French landed on the Isle of Wight and sacked Rye, Lewes, Folkestone and Portsmouth, a poll tax of 4d was introduced. This was payable by every adult under the age of sixty, except beggars, and brought in £22,000. It was generally accepted, however grudgingly, as an unavoidable war tax for a real threat to the defence of the realm.

**John of Gaunt**  Edward III died that same year and was succeeded by his grandson, the ten-year-old Richard II. During his minority, Richard came under the influence of his uncle, John of Gaunt, who withdrew from court to manipulate politics from behind the scenes. Gaunt was a great landowner in the north of England, the Midlands and Gascony. His retinue numbered some 200 barons, knights and squires. Towards the end of Edward's reign, he had wielded considerable power in Parliament, but was neither liked nor trusted. In fact, he was so hated by the public at large that his servants were afraid to be seen wearing his livery. He aroused further anger when, a year after the first poll tax, he led an unsuccessful assault on France and demanded that Parliament should grant a second tax to help fund it.

In 1379 a further incursion into French territory was already being planned. Simon Sudbury, Archbishop of Canterbury and Richard's new lord chancellor, asked Parliament for £160,000 – a staggering sum of money in the fourteenth century. The English army, he argued, was stranded, unable to pay wages and

Richard II was crowned in 1377, at the age of ten. When the Peasants' Revolt broke out four years later, the rebels' anger was not directed at him but at his advisers – whom they suspected were lining their pockets with the crippling poll tax money.

in danger of a humiliating defeat by France. As a result, Parliament imposed a third poll tax in 1380. At a shilling a head for every person between fifteen and sixty years old, it was three times higher than the poll tax of 1377 and fell heavily on those who were the least able to pay. The treasurer, Thomas Brantingham, Bishop of Exeter, resigned (or was perhaps dismissed) and was replaced by Sir Robert Hales.

The immediate response to the tax was evasion. There **Tax evasion** was a dramatic drop in the number of names recorded in the official rolls – a discrepancy of nearly 460,000 between the first poll tax of 1377 and the final one of 1380. Collusion between tax inspectors and villagers was suspected. As a result, special commissioners were appointed to verify the situation, and it was reported that 13,000 suppressed names were collected in Suffolk alone in a matter of weeks. The bullying tactics and gross behaviour of the commissioners stirred up hatred. So much anger was brewing that the tax collectors of London and Middlesex refused to carry out a third census, saying that it was too dangerous.

Although the causes of the Peasants' Revolt were varied – perhaps even influenced by the peasants' uprising in northern France, the brutally suppressed Jacquerie of 1358 – contemporary chroniclers were agreed that it was the third poll tax, along with the insulting behaviour of the commissioners who collected it, that proved to be the breaking point. As the Evesham chronicler recorded: 'This enaction was the cause of the unheard-of evil which followed.' The common people did not trust the courtiers who were advising the young King Richard. Most despised of all were John of Gaunt, Simon Sudbury and the newly appointed treasurer, Sir Robert Hales – all allegedly getting rich on their hefty taxes.

## The Peasants' Revolt of 1381

On 30 May 1381, a royal official named John Bampton, former sheriff of Essex, unsuspectingly rode into Brentwood to investigate the non-payment of the poll tax. He was accompanied by three clerks and two sergeants-at-arms. A table was put up in the village square and Bampton began to cross-question representatives of the marshland villages of Fobbing, Stanford-le-Hope and Corringham. Thomas Baker, a baker by trade as his name suggests, stepped out of the crowd to declare that the taxes had been paid and no more would be forthcoming. When the sergeants-at-arms tried to arrest him, a hundred peasants rounded on them. Bruised, battered and severely frightened, the tax collectors fled.

The next day, Sir Robert Bealknap, Chief Justice of Common Pleas, was sent with three local jurors and three clerks to round up and try the insurgents. This time there was a reception committee awaiting them of some 500 armed peasants. Bealknap was tied back to front on his horse and driven out of town. The jurors and clerks were beheaded, their heads mounted on poles and paraded in the local villages.

In spite of sanctions such as the stocks, the poll tax of 1380 was met with evasion, then violence.

Preparations must have been laid ahead, as the next we hear is that the Essex rioters set off southwards to the fearsome fortress of Rochester Castle, in Kent, where they were joined by a huge local contingent. The chroniclers record that the horde was now 50,000 strong. The *Anonimalle Chronicle* reveals what happened next: 'They laid strong siege on the castle, and the constable defended himself vigorously for half a day, but at length for fear that he had of such tumult, and because of the mad multitude of folks from Essex and Kent, he yielded to them.'

**John Ball &**
**Wat Tyler**

They then broke into the dungeons and released the prisoners. Encouraged by their success, they forged on to Maidstone, about 14 kilometres/9 miles further south. Their aim was to release John Ball, the 'mad priest of Kent', imprisoned there

English troops landing in Normandy, from a French chronicle of the fourteenth century. England's territories in France were a cause of tension until 1453.

by Archbishop Sudbury. Ball was an excommunicated and fundamentalist priest, known and much punished for his anti-establishment rhetoric. Once freed, he became one of the leaders of the uprising and harangued the rebels daily with his radical socialist views in the Lollard tradition. He incited them to 'chastise well Hobbe the Robber', a reference in riddle form to Robert Hales, the hated treasurer. His famous sermon on social equality, delivered at Blackheath on 13 June, inspired future rebels and is still quoted today: 'When Adam delved and Eve span, who was then the gentleman?' Men were later hanged simply for having one of Ball's letters in their pockets.

Little is known about the lives of the other two leaders, Jack Straw, who headed the Essex men, or Wat Tyler from Kent – although Tyler is thought to have served in the war against France, and *Froissart's Chronicle* says 'he was indeed a tiler of houses'. On 10 June, Tyler led 4,000 rebels into Canterbury and stormed the cathedral during high mass. They demanded Sudbury's head but on finding that he was not there, they warned the terrified monks to prepare themselves for a new archbishop – John Ball. Other 'traitors' were tracked down in the town and beheaded. The dissidents burned and ransacked the home of the controller of John of Gaunt's household, and that of the under-treasurer. They rounded on the sheriff of Kent and destroyed the tax rolls.

Heading north-west for London, they reached Blackheath at speed, arriving there the following evening. An advanced guard of the Kent group broke open Marshalsea prison, burned down the warden's house and, according to the *Anonimalle Chronicle*, 'released from prison all the men held there for debt or felonies'. The chronicle describes how they next swooped on to Archbishop Sudbury's Palace at Lambeth, 'set fire to most of its abandoned contents', 'stove in wine barrels' and 'banged together and smashed all the kitchenware'.

Meanwhile Jack Straw was leading his men to London from Essex. His first target was the priory owned by the Knights of St John, in Clerkenwell, where Sir Robert Hales was prior. As the *Westminster Chronicle* records, they not only burned down the building but were 'killing everybody who offered opposition'. By 12 June, thousands of rebels had taken up position on opposite sides of the River Thames – the Essex men in Aldgate, close to the City of London, and the Kent contingent at Blackheath.

The chroniclers express amazement at the government's apathy up to this point. No action had been taken in the fortnight since the troubles started. However, the army was in France, leaving few forces at the government's disposal apart from 600 of the king's men-at-arms and some archers. Richard II and his advisers held a belated council of war in the Tower of London to discuss their options. A messenger was sent to find out what the rebels wanted. The grim reply was delivered by a knight captured by the insurgents: 'to save the king and to destroy the traitors to him and the kingdom'.

**Blackheath** The king and his entourage decided to negotiate. It was arranged for Richard to meet the rebels on the shore below Blackheath. A small royal party set out by boat from the Tower of London to be confronted by a dense crowd of 10,000 peasants, banners of St George and pennants fluttering. Since it was considered too dangerous for the fourteen-year-old king to leave the boat, the crowds were asked to make their demands from a safe distance. They refused, demanding that the king land, but instead the royal party retreated. Although the rebels shouted 'treason' in anger, they made no attempt to release their lethal longbows. However, this failed meeting made them even more determined to push forward into London and to be heard.

They crossed the river into the city effortlessly thanks to a sympathetic alderman, John Horn, who lowered London Bridge contrary to his strictest orders. Assuring the Kent rebels that London would welcome them, he procured a royal banner and headed their march himself. It is recorded that the peasants advanced in an orderly fashion, divided into groups by village or town. To the north, Aldgate was opened to the Essex rebels without argument by another sympathetic (or fearful) alderman. Although the majority of the rebels were peasants and the poor of London, among them were also some local government officials, tax inspectors, village constables and bailiffs, clerks and friars, knights, gentry and aldermen.

The Kent rebels had certain targets clearly in mind, including the Savoy – the sumptuous palace of John of Gaunt – and the Fleet prison. Another was the Temple, which represented not only the hated law but, as part of the Order of St John, was also associated with the treasurer, Sir Robert Hales. A contemporary account describes how the horde 'pulled down the houses and ripped off all the tiles so that the houses were left roofless and derelict. They went to the church and took all the books, rolls and remembrances kept in the cupboards of the apprentices of the law in the Temple, and carried them to the high road and burnt them.' They also set fire to some neighbouring buildings belonging to a marshall and a chandler.

The chief justice of the King's Bench was beheaded, along with a number of unfortunate judges and law students caught at random. One chronicler remarked of the lawyers that it was marvellous to see 'how even the most aged and infirm of them scrambled off, with the agility of rats or evil spirits'.

The Savoy, the rebels' prime target, was described as a building 'incomparable in nobility and beauty', with orchards and fishponds that extended down to the Thames. John of Gaunt was away, so escaped harm, but the rioters broke into the palace, says the *Anonimalle Chronicle*, and 'tore the golden cloths and silk hangings to pieces and crushed them underfoot; they ground up jewels and other rings inlaid with precious stones in small mortars, so that they could never be used again.'

They stormed the prisons of Westminster and Newgate, and

many of the released prisoners joined the revolt. At the church of St Martin's-le-Grand they tore a magistrate away from the altar, dragged him to Cheapside and beheaded him. That day, eighteen other people were decapitated and their heads displayed on London Bridge.

The rebels camped at St Katharine's Dock, nearby the Tower of London, to make sure that no one from the royal party could slip away. From the Tower, king and council watched the smoke of the dying fires and heard the crowds below clamouring for the heads of the 'traitors'. A knight was sent into the camp to read another royal message, offering a general pardon to everyone involved in the uprising, and asking each man to 'return home and set down his grievance in writing'. The king would then take the advice of his lords and 'provide such remedy as will be profitable to himself, his commons and the whole realm'. The rebels' response was that this was all 'trifles and mockery'. The knight was told to return with a better answer.

At this point king and council decided to take a gamble. Knowing that the people meant no harm to Richard, whom they believed was appointed by God and was with them as 'King Richard and the true commons', it was agreed that the king would meet them the following day at Mile End, a village surrounded by open fields outside the city walls.

That night Tyler and the other leaders came up with a new wide-ranging political manifesto – freedom for the serfs, an end to bondage and the right for peasants to sell their produce where they chose. Land rent would be fixed at 4d an acre throughout the country. All legislation since the Black Death would be repealed. The Church would be dismantled, leaving John Ball as England's only bishop, at the head of the parish priests. Church land would be confiscated. And the rebels would not be punished.

**Mile End**   At 7a.m. on 14 June King Richard rode out to Mile End for his second meeting with the rebels. Some of the crowds, amounting to 100,000, surrounded his small retinue and grabbed at the reins. Two of the lords, his half-brothers, broke ranks and fled. However, when the king arrived at the meeting point, the rebels knelt

John Ball, on horseback, haranguing the Kent and Essex rioters who proudly carry the banners of England and St George. From *Froissart's Chronicles.*

and greeted him with words of loyalty: 'Well met our King Richard, if it please you we want no king except yourself.' Tyler presented him with the petition, and Richard cunningly agreed to their demands, which included the abolition of serfdom. He had thirty monks draw up charters, which were stamped with the Great Seal of England and given to a representative of each county that day, along with a banner as royal protection. Most of the Essex men set off home, content with their charters full of false royal promises.

Wat Tyler and his Kent contingent, however, were not to be diverted from breaking into the Tower to punish Richard's ministers and advisers. This was possible because the drawbridge was still down and the portcullis raised, following the king's departure that morning. The *St Albans Chronicle* of Thomas Walsingham records with distaste: 'who would ever have believed that

**Tower of London**

such rustics, and most inferior ones at that, would dare (not in crowds but individually) to enter the chamber of the king and of his mother with their filthy sticks ... The rebels, who had formerly belonged to the most lowly condition of serf, went in and out like lords; and swineherds set themselves above soldiers.'

Archbishop Sudbury, who had taken refuge in the Tower, attempted escape but was foiled. He, along with Robert Hales, a Franciscan friar who was John of Gaunt's physician, and a tax collector from Middlesex, among others, were dragged to the block and beheaded on Tower Hill. Their heads were stuck on poles and paraded to London Bridge. Sudbury's head was placed at the front of the procession, a red cap secured to his skull with a nail.

The Tower of London, originally built by William the Conqueror as his personal fortress, was a symbol of royal power. The rebels were determined to enter and seize Archbishop Sudbury and other hated figures.

The rebel leaders took the moral high ground as 'zealots for truth and justice', and punished anyone caught looting. But by now discipline had become lax, and murder and arson continued throughout 14 June. Old scores started to be settled. The Londoners were bent on taking revenge on the Flemish weavers whom they thought were stealing their jobs. At London Bridge they attacked a 'house of stews' (owned by the Mayor of London, William Walworth) and killed the Flemish prostitutes. Later they were to kill thirty-five innocent Flemings in the street. Anyone who could not say 'bread and cheese' in an English accent was fair game. Others among the rebels asked the question 'With whom hold you?'. If the answer was not the slogan 'With King Richard and the true commons', swift and brutal death would ensue. It was reckoned that in total 140 to 160 people were beheaded that day alone.

The king agreed to meet the rebels once again, this time in Smithfield cattle market. This extraordinary event proved to be a turning point in the uprising, causing the downfall of Wat Tyler and leading to a period of unrelenting royal retribution. The king and his escort of some 200 men gathered in front of St Bartholomew's Church on 15 June, while Tyler's men, running into many thousands, were lined up on the other side of the square. The *Anonimalle Chronicle* relates:

'And when he was summoned by the mayor in the name of 'Wat Tyler of Maidstone' he came to the king with proud bearing, mounted on a little horse in full view of the commons and dismounted carrying a dagger in his hand ... and once he had got down from the horse, he took the king by the hand and, on half-bended knee, he shook him firmly, and for a long time by the arm, saying to him 'Brother, be of good comfort and joyful, for in the next fortnight you will have forty thousand more of the commons than you have at the moment, and we shall be good companions.'

It would seem that the king was somewhat puzzled by these words, as his only response was to ask why Tyler would not go back to his 'own country'. This incensed Tyler. The *Anonimalle Chronicle* continues: 'The said Wat Tyler demanded a jug of water ... and then he proceeded to rinse out his mouth in a gross and disgusting way in front of the king and he demanded a jug of ale, which he downed in a great mouthful.' He then remounted his horse. The chronicler Henry Knighton tells how 'He stood close to the king, speaking for the others, and carrying an unsheathed knife, the kind people call a dagger, which he tossed from hand to hand as a child might play with it, and looked as though he might suddenly seize the opportunity to stab the king if he should refuse their requests.'

Some believe that Wat Tyler was then deliberately provoked. According to the *Anonimalle Chronicle*, one of the king's valets stepped out to accuse Tyler of being 'the greatest thief and robber in all Kent'. Tyler tried to strike the valet with his dagger, and in the scuffle that ensued was mortally wounded. His horse carried him off into the crowd, where he was heard 'crying to the commons to

After one of the king's household runs Wat Tyler through with a sword (shown on the left), Richard turns to address and calm the agitated rebels. (*Froissart's Chronicles*).

avenge him' before falling to the ground half dead.

Richard, the boy king, showed remarkable courage and presence of mind in the face of the hostile mass of rebels. He rode forward to address them and, to buy himself time, commanded them to meet him at Clerkenwell Fields. The mayor hurried back to the City and, as Thomas Walsingham recounts, raised a 'company of well-armed folks' who 'enveloped the commons like sheep within a pen'. The mayor then returned to Smithfield, 'to make an end of the captain of the commons'. Tyler, who may already have been dead, was beheaded. His head was set on a pole and taken to the king at Clerkenwell.

The loss of their leader brought the uprising to an end. Walsingham describes the scene: 'And when the commons saw that their chieftain, Wat Tyler, was dead in such a manner, they fell to the ground there among the wheat, like beaten men, imploring the king for mercy for their misdeeds. And the king benevolently granted them mercy, and most of them took to flight.'

However, the king's mercy was short-lived. Having outwitted the rebels, he lost no time in taking his revenge. An army was sent into Essex to crush the rebels there, killing some 500 peasants at a battle in Billericay on 28 June. On 2 July an order was issued cancelling the charters in which the king had granted the serfs freedom. Richard sent out messengers 'to capture the malefactors and put them to death', as the *Anonimalle Chronicle* records. He took a large army and went into the rebellious villages, telling the people that they would come to no harm if they named the ringleaders. John Ball was caught in Coventry. He was hung, drawn and quartered there in front of Richard on 15 July. Although revolts continued in Leicester, Suffolk, Norfolk and Cambridgeshire, by autumn all were quelled. When finally Richard called a halt to the bloodshed and law was restored, his message to the people was chilling. 'Rustics you were and rustics you are still; you will remain in bondage, not as before but incomparably harsher.'

The Peasants' Revolt had almost overturned the government in a matter of weeks. Both the chancellor and the chief justice had been murdered. Had he not been in Scotland at the time, John of Gaunt, the king's uncle, would have certainly met the same fate. Quantities of irreplaceable legal records and royal papers in the hallowed vaults of such places as the Temple and Lambeth Palace had been destroyed.

Wat Tyler, John Ball and Jack Straw were to become the stuff of legends as the first commoners to actually threaten the political structures of their day. They had shown that downtrodden commoners, mere peasants, could rock the very establishment. The Great Uprising set the liberating precedent for future peasant revolts. For the first time, the voice of the common people had been heard loud and clear throughout the land. Although the rising failed in its somewhat unrealistic objectives at the time, one thing is for sure. In the long term it contributed to freeing the serf from the much-resented 'Norman yoke'.

# 3. WOOL, THE THEFT OF THE COMMONS & THE PARISH WORKHOUSE 1500–1800

'I praise God and ever shall
It is the sheep hath paid for all.'
Inscription from the mansion of John Barton,
wool merchant, Nottinghamshire

By the end of the sixteenth century, serfdom was extinct in Britain. The shortage of labour caused by the Black Death in the fourteenth century had brought about a swing from arable to less labour-intensive – and far more lucrative – sheep farming. In the consequent scramble to enclose, landowners began to skirt, even flout, the law. They made private arrangements to take over the commons, evict their tenants, wipe out villages, and enclose the land for themselves. Although the Tudors and early Stuarts upheld the laws that preserved the commons, they finally gave in to what they saw as the inevitable when their last anti-enclosure bill was defeated in 1656. A new era of parliamentary enclosures lay ahead.

The 'fair field full of folk' so evocatively described in Langland's *Piers Plowman* was being replaced by fields full of sheep. Many labourers and their families, having lost their homes and livelihoods, became penniless vagrants. An added misfortune for the peasants was that Henry VIII's dissolution of the monasteries in the mid-sixteenth century removed the main source of alms to the poor. To deal with the problem of widespread pauperism, Elizabeth I brought in an apprentice system and made parishes responsible for the 'deserving poor'. Workhouses and houses of correction were founded.

Later legislation did little more than ward off starvation.

Elizabeth I also introduced the far-sighted Planning Act of 1589. This required all new cottages to have enough land attached for a degree of self-sufficiency – a buffer to forestall any necessity of seeking help. The law was not put into practice at the time but the idea re-emerged two centuries later, during the Allotment Movement of the late eighteenth century.

## Wool & the glint of gold

'The most striking single aspect of the English landscape at the beginning of the sixteenth century,' wrote William George Hoskins in his book *The Making of the English Landcape* (1955), 'was that there were about three sheep to every human being' – some eight million

The fourteenth-century Luttrell Psalter is illustrated with scenes of rural life and work. Here, sheep are being milked – but even more valuable was their wool, exported to Florence and other European cities.

according to his estimate. There was good reason for this, as English wool was highly esteemed. It had paid a king's ransom, securing the release of Richard the Lionheart in the twelfth century, and also largely funded the battles launched against the French by the three King Edwards between 1272 and 1377. In gratitude to the fortunes that wool had brought the country, Edward III had decreed that the seat for his lord chancellor should be made from a woolsack.

The Sumptuary Law of 1363 shows the historic importance attached to the wool trade. With the aim of discouraging **Woollen shrouds** imports, it laid down the types of clothing permitted for each level of society. For 'carters, ploughmen, drivers of the plough, oxherds, cowherds, shepherds, dairy workers and all other keepers of beasts', it prohibited 'any manner of cloth but blanket and russet wool of 12d'. In 1666, however, demand for wool slumped as silks and linens became more fashionable, causing distress in the cottage industries. To deal with the resulting glut of wool, and for 'the encouragement of the woollen manufacturer', an act was passed requiring that no corpse should be buried in anything other than English wool. Those too poor for a shroud would have the coffin marked 'naked'.

Most of the wool came from the great landowners and the wealthy Cistercian and Augustinian monasteries. The Cistercians, in particular, drained large tracts of marshland and cleared forests to make prairie-sized pastures. The buyers and their agents from abroad put in vast orders and drew up contracts many years in advance. The wool of the small shorthaired mountain sheep from the poor pastures of the Welsh and Scottish borders made the finest soft woollen yarn. The larger, longwool Cotswold, Lincoln and Leicester breeds, feeding on lusher pastures, produced top-quality wool for worsteds and serge. Both were highly sought after by the finest cloth manufacturers based in Bruges, Ghent, Ypres and Florence.

Their cloth and tailored clothes were later rivalled by those of English weavers. The standard of craftsmanship was high, as Queen Elizabeth's 1562 Statute of Artificers demanded a seven-year apprenticeship. Wages were set by a Justice of the Peace, with the assistance of the sheriff if available. To give or accept higher wages was against the law. Apprentices could not leave their employment without a certificate.

While the wool merchants and sheep farmers made their fortunes, by the sixteenth century many lords of the manor were finding themselves strapped for cash and forced to sell up. According to James Harrington in *The Commonwealth of Oceana* (1656), the nobility spent much time at court because tired of country life, and their revenues 'never to have been exhausted by beef and mutton, were found narrow, whence followed racking of rents, and at length sale of lands'. The extravagance of Henry VIII (1491–1547) had set a bad example. Edward Chamberlayne complained about widespread self-indulgence in *Angliae Notitiae, or, The Present State of England* (1669). 'The English,' he says, 'especially the gentry, are so much

As great landowners and sheep farmers, the monasteries produced much of England's prized wool. They often sold it several years ahead, signing advance contracts with foreign merchants.

given to prodigality and slothfulness, that estates are oftener spent and sold than in any other country.' So free are they with money that not only 'cooks, vintners, innkeepers, and such mean fellows, enrich themselves and beggar and insult over the gentry', but even 'tailors, dancing masters and such trifling fellows arrive to that riches and pride, as to ride in their coaches, keep their summer houses, to be served in plate, etc. an insolence insupportable in other well-governed nations.'

Unlike the nobles, the yeomen were hands-on farmers – and far too shrewd to squander their money. Among them was being forged a new and powerful middle class. The diplomat and scholar Sir Thomas Smith, author of *De Republica Anglorum*, noted in the 1560s that it was the yeomen who were buying up the lands of 'unthrifty gentlemen'. A century later, Thomas Fuller, clergyman, commented in his *History of the Worthies of England* (1662) that the yeomanry were 'an estate of people almost peculiar to England'. The typical yeoman, he observes, 'wears russet clothes,

**Rise of the yeoman**

but makes golden payment, having tin in his buttons and silver in his pocket'. Described as a class of 'forty shilling freeholders', in reference to the value of the land or property they held, they often fulfilled communal responsibilities as jurymen, churchwardens and overseers of the poor.

At the bottom of the social scale, the descendants of the medieval villeins were described by William Harrison, canon of Windsor and author of *Description of Elizabethan England* (1577), as those who had 'neither voice nor authority in the commonwealth, but are to be ruled and not to rule other[s]'.

**The landless labourer**

Labourers, stripped of their manorial rights, were increasingly becoming landless farm workers only worth what they were paid for hire by the day, the week, or by results. Some would be employed for specialist tasks – hedging, shearing or wood clearance. Others might be employed for 'harvest month' on a wage that included meals, possibly with some gleaning thrown in. More were hired casually in gangs for menial work – weeding, field clearance or fruit-picking.

Work as a farm servant was more secure. Engaged by the year, servants lived, worked and ate with the family. A large estate might employ a bailiff, carter, ploughman, shepherd, cowherd, thresher, 'first' and 'second' man, and dairymaids. Hiring fairs, introduced by

**Mop fairs**

Edward III in his 1351 Statute of Labourers, were known as 'staties', or 'mop fairs' because of the tassel worn by prospective employees to signify their trade. Shepherds would have a strand of wool, carters some whipcord, and cowmen a few cow hairs.

Twelve scenes, one for each month, to show the peasants' year-long labours out in the fields.

Once hired, these 'mops' were replaced with brightly coloured ribbons as proof of the fact. A 'hiring penny' would pass hands to seal the deal. The fairs took place in market towns at Martinmas, in November, and were festive occasions drawing big crowds.

### The theft of the commons

The law locks up the man or woman
Who steals the goose from off the common
But lets the greater felon loose
Who steals the common from off the goose.
*Anon.*

The lower orders of society were not without their sympathizers. John Fitzherbert from Derbyshire, author of the *Book of Husbandry* (1523), had warned that the effect of enclosure would be unemployment and depopulation, as well as the destruction of villages. He recommended mixed husbandry: a man cannot thrive by corn unless he has livestock, and he who tries to keep stock without corn is either 'a buyer, a borrower or a beggar'. Both Cardinal Wolsey and Sir Thomas More, lord chancellors and advisers to Henry VIII, attempted to ban the enclosure of the commons for sheep rearing. In his book *Utopia* (1516), More comments drily on the foolish greed among the gentry and 'certain abbots': "your sheep that were wont to be so meek and tame, and so small eaters, now, as I heard say, be become so great devourers and so wild, that they eat up, and swallow down the very men themselves. They consume, destroy, and devour whole fields, houses, and cities. For . . . noble men, and gentlemen, yea and certain abbots, holy men no doubt, not contenting themselves with the yearly revenues and profits . . . leave no ground for tillage: they enclose all into pastures, they throw down houses, they pluck down towns, and leave nothing standing, but only the church to be made a sheephouse.'

**Old Enclosed**  By the sixteenth century, the wealthier farmers, including the ever-more prosperous yeomen as well as the gentry, were coming to private arrangements on joint enclosures and

Sir Thomas More (1478–1535) denounced the vast enclosure of the commons for sheep rearing, blaming the depopulation of villages and loss of work on arable land for social problems such as theft and vagrancy.

sharing out the common land among themselves. These often involved the rearrangement of open-field strips into single small farmsteads. Commissioners were appointed by the interested parties to see fair play. Lawyers and surveyors would have been engaged. These early enclosures by agreement – an 'agreement of the most part of the better sort' – became known as 'Old Enclosed,' as opposed to the wave of parliamentary enclosures that took place from the 1750s.

The Tudors and early Stuarts made considerable efforts to stem this tide by upholding and reinforcing the laws that protected the commons. Their concerns were that a loss of arable land and consequent decrease in grain production would make the country more susceptible to famine and lead to higher prices for imports. They feared revolution. A law passed in 1489 – while not outlawing enclosure – sought to deter it by decreeing that half of any profits made from pulling down houses would go to the Crown until the houses had been rebuilt. In 1515 conversion from arable to pasture became an offence in the same way and with the same penalty attached, that half the profits would go to the Crown until the land was restored to its original use.

In 1517, Cardinal Wolsey launched a national enquiry to determine where illegal enclosures had taken place and to ensure that the Crown received its rightful share of the profits. Many wealthy landowners were brought to court and were

**Wolsey's enquiry**

made to rebuild villages and restore land to arable farming. Needless to say, this made the cardinal deeply unpopular with the aristocracy and also, unfortunately, had little effect on stemming the tide. The gentry still had some clout, and in 1529 Wolsey was forced to accept that all existing enclosures would remain.

Nonetheless, in 1533 a further act to restrict sheep farming was introduced and in 1548 the Privy Council, led by Edward Seymour, Protector Somerset, declared on behalf of the eleven-year-old Edward VI that enclosure was a 'moral evil'. Although Somerset described the commoners as 'inferiors to brute beasts', he nevertheless enforced laws to protect the commons. He decreed that local commissioners should be made responsible for tracking down and removing the recent enclosures of 'covetous' landowners. He also feared that trouble was brewing among the 'naughtie papist priests'. They were leading some of the anti-

The court of the King's Bench, at Westminster, heard cases involving the Crown's interests. In local disputes, settled by manorial courts or quarter sessions, landowners wanting to create enclosures found ways round the law.

enclosure revolts and, so he believed, were plotting behind his back.

During Elizabeth I's reign, the 1563 Tillage Act for the 'maintenance of husbandry and tillage' aimed to prevent the conversion of arable to pasture in order to curb 'idleness, drunkenness, unlawful games and all other lewd practices'. Despite all efforts, however, the cottagers continued to be displaced and many were facing ruin. During local negotiations for enclosure, the uneducated peasants might be short-changed with some compensation, providing they had legal rights,

Many displaced labourers, lacking any means of support, joined the bands of strolling players and gypsies. Elizabethan laws, brought in to counter the threat of social disorder, dealt harshly with the 'undeserving poor'.

or evicted, empty-handed, if not. Belonging to 'the rabble that cannot read', they were at a distinct disadvantage when trying to make their case and might be intimidated or hoodwinked into signing their rights away. Where the lord was absent, the newly wealthy villagers might conspire against their poor or landless neighbours.

**Loopholes in the law**

There were ways round the law, particularly since the law enforcers were themselves of the landowning class, and loopholes also existed that allowed landlords to evict their tenants. To remove non-hereditary copyholders (a form of tenure based on manorial records), the landlord merely had to wait for the existing tenant to die before giving notice to his heirs. The hereditary copyholders included those with a non-fixed rent, or 'fine'. The landlord could legally raise the rent so high that the tenants had no choice but to leave. Even when decisions had been made in favour of cottagers by the manor court, landowners would sometimes simply override them and get away with it.

Gypsy with mandolin.

**The Court of Star Chamber**

The power of the manor courts was in decline at this period. Matters were increasingly settled at the county quarter sessions, presided over by two Justices of the Peace with a jury. Crimes with capital sentences, though, were heard at the assizes, the periodical criminal courts. Questions of property rights and enclosure, also rioting, strikes, and criticism (even jokes) against the king, often came under the king's aegis at Westminster, where they were heard at the Court of Star Chamber, or *Camera Stellata* (named

Cottagers turned out of their homes often resorted to putting up makeshift shelters or 'hovels' on waste ground.

for its star-spangled ceiling), until it was abolished in 1641. Later they were held at the court of the King's Bench, where the judges were selected from among the king's privy councillors to protect his interests and those of the commoners.

## The parish workhouse

Rural labourers were powerless to prevent enclosure and had no protection from its consequences, particularly since events at the start of the sixteenth century had removed their only safety net in times of poverty.

In 1534 Henry VIII broke from Rome with the Act of Supremacy, declaring that he recognized 'no superior in earth, but only God'. The dissolution of the monasteries that followed changed the British landscape irrevocably. Many monasteries were torn down or blown up with gunpowder, their contents sold

**Dissolution of the monasteries**

to the highest bidder at auction. Much monastic land fell into the hands of unscrupulous speculators. Henry profited by the best part of £1 million, but along with the demise of the monasteries many charitable almshouses and hospitals were lost. How to deal with the poor – and who should pay – was left to Henry's successors to tackle. It was a problem that resounded into the nineteenth century.

**Cotters and squatters**
Evicted cottagers and squatters were often reduced to building rough dwellings, referred to as hovels, on the waste ground of villages. The manorial records are full of encroachments, 'purpestres', which were sometimes allowed on payment of a small fine and providing it 'doth no hurt' according to the custom of the manor. Dwellings put up between sunset and dawn were permitted to stay if there was smoke coming out of the chimney the next morning – a challenge, to say the least.

Under Elizabeth I, the 1589 Planning Act against Erecting and Maintaining Cottages was aimed at protecting employment for local people and reducing poverty due to the over-population of villages. It required all new cottages to have 1.6 hectares/4 acres of land attached so that the inhabitants could maintain themselves 'and not be obliged on the loss of a few days' labour to come to the parish'. The concept of providing land for self-sufficiency was ahead of its time but was not widely adopted.

Labourers were allowed to apply for work and settle within 1.6 kilometres/1 mile of mines and quarries, market towns and maritime districts – places where there was work to spare. Many joined the bands of itinerant merchants, craftsmen, pedlars, strolling players,

**Beggars and vagrants**
artisans, gypsies and clowns. Beggars and 'rogues forlorn' were a common sight. Robbers and outlaws joined with the destitute, sometimes extracting alms with the 'beggar's curse'. As this old rhyme suggests, outsiders were not always welcome:

Hark, hark the dogs do bark: the beggars are coming to town.
Some gave them white bread, and some gave them brown,
And some gave them a good horsewhip and sent them out of town.

In the Middle Ages, those begging without a licence were liable to suffer ingenious punishments, such as 'burning through the gristle of the right ear'. Homelessness classed people as vagabonds – not a desirable position in life, as it brought both punishment and disgrace. Under the Act against Vagabonds and Beggars of 1495, the punishment was three days in the stocks on bread and water, followed by expulsion. In 1597 it was decreed that a 'sturdy beggar' be stripped to the waist and 'whipped until bloody' before being expelled and sent back to the parish of his birth. The poor were commonly 'badged' and made to wear shaming ribbons.

The Elizabethan Poor Law of 1601 made parishes **Poor Law** responsible for their own paupers. The law defined different categories of poor people and discriminated heavily against the 'idle poor', who were able-bodied but refused to work. They were forced into the prison-like houses of correction to mend their ways at hard labour, while the 'deserving poor' were provided with 'outdoor relief' in the form of the parish loaf, as decreed by Justices of the Peace. Overseers administered the provision of housing, feeding, medical attention and burial.

This system came to be seen as unfair, as the more generous parishes attracted greater numbers of poor people, causing distress among the residents who were burdened with paying the poor rates. In addition, whereas in the early seventeenth century villages had been small enough for everyone to know each other, as the population increased and people moved away from their homes, the poor laws became harder to administer.

The 1662 Settlement and Removal Act was an attempt to **Settlement &** solve this set of problems by pinning the poor down in their **Removal Act** place of residence. It required people to prove 'settlement' before they could claim poor relief. To qualify, applicants had to have been employed by an established resident for more than a year and a day (which led to many contracts that fell just short of the year), have been born there, have lived there for more than three years, held parish office, rented property for more than £10 a year, be married to a parish resident, or have served a full seven-year apprenticeship.

Intensely cruel punishments, particularly for treason, but also for minor offences, carried on well into the Elizabethan era.

Once someone had taken the risk of leaving their own village to chance their luck elsewhere, it was almost impossible in practical terms to get a 'settlement certificate' to guarantee that their home parish would pay for their return, or removal, should they need poor relief at some future date. Without this certificate they would have to find their own way back, no matter how old or sick, to get any poor relief whatsoever. The effect of the law was to trap the poor in their villages and discourage them from trying to find work elsewhere.

Adam Smith, the economist and author of the *Wealth of Nations*, pointed out in 1776 that 'To remove a man who has committed no misdemeanour from the parish where he chooses to reside, is an evident violation of natural liberty and justice.' In 1797, the law was slightly modified so that no one seriously ill should be removed, nor anyone who had not yet become a charge on the rates. Nonetheless, a contemporary historian wrote that it had led to 'a greater quantity of litigation and hostile divisions than any other law on the statute book – aye, or than all the other laws from the time of the Magna Carta put together'.

In a further attempt to reduce the cost of the poor rates, the 1723 Workhouse Test Act, otherwise known as Knatchbull's Act, encouraged parishes to set up new workhouses, and decreed that anyone refusing a place would be 'put out of the parish books' and no longer be eligible for poor relief. Able-bodied applicants were put to the test to ensure that they were not shirkers and wasting the poor rates. Typical tasks would include stone crushing for roads, bone crushing, or oakum picking (pulling apart old tar-soaked ship's ropes). To discourage any but the truly desperate, conditions were made as humiliating and unpleasant as possible, as captured by George Crabbe, poet of the poor, in 'The Parish Workhouse' (1783): **Knatchbull's Act**

> There, where the putrid vapours flagging play,
> And the dull wheel hums doleful through the day;
> There children dwell who know no parents' care;
> Parents, who know no children's love, dwell there;
> Heart-broken matrons on their joyless bed,
> Forsaken wives and mothers never wed;
> Dejected widows with unheeded tears,
> And crippled age with more than childhood-fears;
> The lame, the blind, and – far the happiest they! –
> The moping idiot and the madman gay.

The first returns showed that 2,000 workhouses had been established in England by 1776. As the costs of providing indoor relief were high, some parishes adopted the more humane Gilbert's Act of 1782 and reserved their workhouses for children, the elderly and infirm. The able-bodied poor were given outdoor relief either in the form of money, food and clothes, or employment near their **Gilbert's Act** homes, in which case local employers received a top-up from parish rates to bring wages up to subsistence levels. Sir Frederick Morton Eden, pioneering author of *The State of the Poor* (1797) described the 'roundsmen' of Kibworth Beauchamp in Leicestershire: 'when a man is out of work, he applied to the overseer who sends him from house to house to get employ: the housekeeper, who employs him, is bound to give him victuals, and 6d a day; and the parish adds 4d a day for the support of his family.' In some cases, money might be advanced to buy a cow if it was deemed that the household would then be able to survive without applying for poor relief.

In other parishes, all those paying rent of over £20 a year were obliged to employ a man for a day and pay him a shilling. It was an ignominious situation for the unemployed labourers. They were either the responsibility of the ratepayers or hired out at below the market rate by the parish as a second-rate deal. Nor did it help their situation that the hiring fairs were in decline. 'If a servant in agriculture leaves his place,' wrote the Rector of Whatfield to the Poor Law Commission in the nineteenth century, 'it is seldom indeed that he can get another except as an occasional day labourer. Labourers now live seldom under their employers' roofs for these reasons: the number of unemployed labourers is such, that a farmer is always sure of hands when he wants them. It is cheaper to hire day labourers … than to maintain servants in the house, especially as they are always sent home on a rainy day.' Farm servants no longer ate with their masters as part of the extended family. As farmers grew wealthier and more gentrified, the gap between man and servant widened. It was noted that 'Now farmers had parlours, labourers are no more found in kitchens.'

**The Speenhamland System**

In 1795, finally some concern was shown for the struggling labourer and his family. The cost of corn had risen due to bad harvests and war with France. At a meeting in the Pelican Inn at Speenhamland, near Newbury, a group of landowners, clergy and justices came up with a novel idea to 'alleviate the distresses of the poor with as little burden on the occupiers of the land as possible'. The plan was that the poor rates should top up wages according to

Hiring fairs were introduced by Edward III in 1351 and continued until the twentieth century. These were festive occasions which, in the seventeenth century, were the main way for employers to find live-in farm servants on a year's contract.

the price of bread. The number would be calculated on three gallon-loaves a week for a working man and half that amount for his wife and children, taking into account wages and the size of his family. The poor of the parish would go in a group to the justices to make their claims and be paid.

The Speenhamland System was adopted across the country (with the exception of Northumberland and Durham) and was to last for forty years. Without doubt it saved many from starvation. The downside was that employers paid as little as they could in the knowledge that wages would be topped up by the parish. The labourer could neither fall below nor rise above bare subsistence levels. He was

The 1562 Elizabethan Statute of Artificers contained many clauses to control labour and repress disorder. Standards of craftsmanship were high, as craftsmen were required to have completed a seven-year apprenticeship.

trapped on the bottom rung. Ratepayers, on the other hand, resented the poor rates as unfair because they fell on all equally, whether or not they benefited from the cheap labour they were subsidizing. Over the years the parishes cut back their expenditure some 30 per cent across the country. One writer noted that 'whereas accepting charity had formerly been a disgrace, it was now demanded as a privilege'.

The rural poor had become the innocent victims of the push for wealth. The peasants felt, with justification, that they were being cast aside and robbed of their ancient rights and their very livelihoods in order to line the pockets of the rich. A government report of 1607 made the astute observation that, for enclosure to work, a balance had to be struck between providing housing for the poor and allowing landowners to pursue improvements in agriculture. However, it seemed beyond them to equate the two. The Tudors were proved right to fear revolution, as the rumblings of discontent against enclosure were about to flare up again.

# 4. THE FIGHT FOR THE RIGHT TO DIG & THE AGRICULTURAL REVOLUTION 1500–1780

'The life of this dark kingly power ... lies within the iron chest of cursed covetousness, who gives the earth to some part of mankind, and denies it to another part of mankind: and that part that hath the earth, hath no right from the law of creation to take it to himself, and shut out others; but he took it away violently by theft and murder in conquest.' Gerrard Winstanley writing after the execution of Charles I, *A New Year's Gift for the Parliament and Army* (1650)

As more land was enclosed, much of it illegally, there were spasmodic rural revolts. One such was the Kett Rebellion of 1549, which started with gangs of frustrated labourers moving from farm to farm tearing down fences, uprooting hedges and filling the ditches that marked the boundaries of the newly enclosed estates. As with the Midland Revolt of 1607, which extended through the enclosure counties of Leicestershire, Northamptonshire and Warwickshire, the Kett Rebellion and other disturbances often ended in pitched battles and were ruthlessly quelled by the military. Sometimes country labourers also joined in the Bread or Blood riots of the cities, in a general protest about their conditions.

Gerrard Winstanley, leader of the True Levellers and a fervent Quaker of the old school, is often referred to as an early communist in the manner of John Ball. Winstanley famously broke into and squatted on private land with his group of followers, where they started to grow vegetables and declared that the land belonged to everyone. This unusual protest took place during the English Civil War of 1642 to 1649, a period of heightened radicalism, dissent and break-off religious sects. Cromwell's highly disciplined New Model Army had a good sprinkling of officers drawn from dissident yeoman landowners and farmers.

The second half of the seventeenth century marks the very beginning of the agricultural revolution, when machines would start to take over from manual labour on the farms. This was to cause further grief to the labourers, who were already struggling to survive. As the noose tightened with the mass parliamentary enclosures that were to follow in the eighteenth century, a movement of wellwishers sprung up to provide land – or rather, to 'allot' it – in what became known as the first Allotment Movement.

## Kett's Rebellion

Robert Kett, a wealthy yeoman farmer and a tanner by trade, had been found guilty of illegally enclosing common land at Wymondham, Norfolk, and was fined by the manorial court. This made him an obvious target for a group of local rebels, who in the summer of 1549 came to fill in his ditches and remove his fences. In what appears to have been an extraordinary change of heart, Kett not only agreed to their demands but helped them tear down the fences around his own land and offered to become their leader. He and his brother William marched with the rebels towards Norwich, setting up camps on their gradual progress along the 16 kilometres/10 miles to the city. They gathered more followers as they went, destroying enclosures, taking prisoners and plundering houses for food and provisions.

Their numbers were further reinforced six weeks later, when they reached the outskirts of Norwich, by the city's poor, whose commons had also been partially enclosed. Now a force some 16,000 strong, the rebels settled at Mousehold Heath, on the north-east of Norwich. With their prisoners safely under lock and key, they opened negotiations with the royal councillors concerning illegal enclosures.

The Rebellion under kett the Tanner in the Oak of Reformation neer Norwich. Pa.149.

Robert Kett holding a council of war with his rebel army at the 'oak of reformation', before they stormed into Norwich in July 1549.

Protector Somerset (uncle and regent to the young Edward VI) sent ambassadors offering a truce, but this was repelled. An officer of the College of Arms was sent to tell them that even though the camp represented 'a rebellion' they would be pardoned as long as they dispersed peacefully. This offer was also rejected.

Five days later the rebels stormed Norwich and took control of the city. The Marquess of Northampton was ordered to raise an army to quell the revolt. A pitched battle followed in the narrow streets, 300 lives were lost and Northampton's army was forced to retreat to Cambridge. A second army, led by the Earl of Warwick, was dispatched. Once more the rebels were offered a royal pardon if they would agree to surrender, to no avail. In the clash that followed this refusal, Kett was forced to retreat to an area outside the city. Undaunted, he continued to make raids on Norwich – until the Battle of Dussindale on 27 August, which ended in heavy defeat. The death toll was some 3,000. Only 350 were on Warwick's side.

Kett and his brother were captured the next day and taken to London for trial at the King's Bench. They were accused of having a rallying cry that incited people to 'kill the gentlemen', and of intending to murder king and court. This was an unlikely charge, as they had protected their prisoners and claimed that their argument was with the gentry for breaking the laws on enclosure. Nevertheless, Robert Kett was found guilty of high treason and of levying war upon the king. He was hanged from the walls of Norwich Castle, having been hauled up to the top of the ramparts alive; his body was left to rot until the flesh fell off his bones. His brother William was hanged in chains from the abbey church of his home town, Wymondham.

## The Midland Revolt of 1607

Some fifty years later, during the reign of James I, revolt was brewing again in the areas where there were the most extensive illegal enclosures – Leicestershire, Northamptonshire and Warwickshire. The 'chiefest leader' of the Midland Revolt was a lowly tinker, John Reynolds, alias Captain Pouch. His nickname sprung from the claim that he could protect his followers with the contents of his leather satchel. He declared that he was invested with authority from the king and the 'Lord of Heaven' to destroy enclosures.

Through his gift for persuasion, in 1607 Captain Pouch gathered some 5,000 followers, 'poor delvers', landless day labourers and craftsmen. He urged them 'not to swear, nor to offer violence to any person, but to ply their business and make fair works' by destroying hedging, filling ditches and breaking into the enclosures of the 'encroaching tyrants' who would grind their flesh on 'the whetstone of poverty'.

Trouble came when the rebels arrived at the property of Thomas Tresham in Newton. Like Kett, he had been prosecuted in court for flouting the law and converting the commons illegally to pasture. He had also bought land from his cousin, Sir Thomas Tresham of Rushton, and had destroyed five farms in order to convert 60 hectares/150 acres of common land into pasture.

As local armed bands and militia were reluctant to fight with their neighbours, landowners were obliged to recruit their own army. A royal proclamation was delivered to the insurgents: they had committed 'seditious libel' in accusing the government of failing to prosecute landlords who had enclosed their land illegally. Disperse or die. A battle ensued. The landowners' cavalry and foot soldiers charged against the rebels, who were now leaderless because Captain Pouch had been arrested the day before. The rioters fought back with stones, bows and arrows, pikes and long bills, but the second charge defeated them. Some forty or more were killed in the battle. Many others were injured or taken prisoner.

There was a trial and the rebels met their usual fate. All that was found in Captain Pouch's magic bag after his execution was a piece of mouldy cheese. However, Robert Wilkinson, chaplain to the Earl of Exeter, gave a sermon during the trial in which he shamed the landlords who had devastated the Northamptonshire countryside with their enclosures and left its people 'in hunger and despair'. As a result of the disturbances, a Royal Commission was set up to look at the extent of illegal enclosure. Their findings reported that 27,000 acres (10,900 hectares) had been wrongfully enclosed, 350 villages demolished and 1,500 people evicted from eighteen villages in the area. Several wealthy landlords were prosecuted and fined, including Thomas Tresham of Newton.

## Civil War

Enclosure, however, not only continued but was soon to increase. The victory of the Parliamentarians over the Royalists in the English Civil War of 1642–1649 made this possible. Many of the parliamentarian leaders themselves were from the newly wealthy yeoman class of landowners and so took the landlords' cause against the interest of the king and the peasants. Many on the side of the royalists, which included much of the gentry, were stripped of their lands. The Star Chamber, which up to then had been the main legal control against the excesses of the enclosing landlords, was abolished. The Civil War also saw the flourishing of a new landowning class, many of whom benefited from the confiscation of Crown lands.

Among the Parliamentarians there was an unexpected **New Model** source of radicalism and dissent: the New Model Army. **Army** Formed in 1645 to provide a more effective prosecution of the war, it was England's first professional army. Under General Fairfax, its upright commander-in-chief between 1645 and 1650, the New Model Army was highly disciplined, motivated, idealistic and refreshingly democratic. Promotion from the ranks was on merit, not class, and several of the army's top men came from humble backgrounds. Oliver Cromwell wrote that he would 'rather have a plain, russet-coated captain that knows what he fights for, and loves what he knows, than that which you call a gentleman and is nothing else.'

Many of the officers were veterans with Puritan beliefs, while many of the conscripted rank and file were dissenters. Among them were represented all kinds of contemporary sects and movements, including Anabaptists, Familists, Quakers, Muggletonians, Barrowists, Brownists, Diggers, Ranters, Sabbatarians and Seekers. Many of the soldiers were Levellers, radical dissenters who advocated equality and religious tolerance (not to be confused with

Thomas Fairfax was the upright commander of the New Model Army. Promotion was on merit not class, and there were many outspoken dissenters among the conscripted ranks. Portrait by Robert Walker.

the agricultural Levellers, so called because they flattened hedges and other enclosure boundaries). As the army moved around the country, including expeditions to Scotland and Ireland, the army's chaplains spread word from the pulpit to the wider populace as much as to their own troops. When Parliament tried to disband the army without settling arrears of pay in 1645, the soldiers elected 'agitators', two per regiment, to lobby for their rights.

It was at around this time that Gerrard Winstanley, a religious reformer and political activist, characterized today as a 'Christian communist', took up the rallying cry uttered by John Ball during the Peasants' Revolt of 1381: 'When Adam delved and Eve span, who was then the gentleman?' Winstanley was the son of a mercer from Wigan, Lancashire. He moved to London in 1630, where he was apprenticed and later became a freeman of the Merchant Taylors' Company. He set up a business but was bankrupted during the Civil War. Bailed out by his father-in-law, Winstanley and his wife Susan went to settle in Cobham, Surrey. There he made a new start as a cowherd, and so had the raw experience of joining the labourers. He was outraged to be fined by the manorial court for harvesting winter fodder and digging up peat without the customary rights of tenants.

Winstanley took up the cause of the landless labourer with religious fervour. He published four theological pamphlets in 1648, followed by *The New Law of Righteousness*, based on the Book of Acts. Having received a message from God, or so he claimed, he advocated equality for all (even women) and anticipated the green movement by condemning enclosures and describing the earth as a 'common storehouse for all', one that should not be 'kept in the hands of a few'. His vision was that 'none shall lay claim to any creature, and say, *This is mine and that is yours, This is my work, that is yours*; but every one shall put to their hands to till the earth and bring up cattle, and the blessing of the earth shall be common to all.'

He perceived Charles I's execution on 30 January 1649 as a victory for the common people, who were now free from the oppressor's 'Norman yoke'. That same year, a small group led by Winstanley and former fellow apprentice, William Everard, a self-styled prophet, broke into the enclosed common land on St George's Hill in Surrey. Calling themselves the True Levellers, they sowed parsnips, carrots and beans to restore 'the ancient community of enjoying the fruits of the earth'. They returned the next day and burned 4 hectares/10 acres of heath. By the end of the week some thirty people were digging all day.

Their activities were not well received. After two months of assaults, intimidation and attempts to get them evicted in the courts, the True Levellers abandoned St George's Hill and tried their luck in neighbouring Cobham. Here John Platt, Rector of West Horsley and lord of the manor at Cobham, rallied anti-Digger support from the locals. The poor tenants who 'durst do no other, because their landlords and lords looked on, for fear they should be turned out of service or their livings' finally drove Winstanley and his companions out, burning the huts and digging up the crops. Other Digger colonies were sent up in Kent, Barnet, Enfield, Buckinghamshire and Northamptonshire on newly enclosed land. Gradually, they too gave up the fight.

## The agricultural revolution

The enclosure rioters could not have imagined that a further threat to their livelihoods was taking shape – the agricultural revolution. By the seventeenth century, research into methods of improving agriculture was pouring in from the Low Countries. The recommendations of 'rustick authors' were compiled into one work by John Worlidge of Petersfield, Hampshire, whose *Systema Agriculturae, or, The Mystery of Husbandry Discovered* (1669) was aimed at the 'gentry and yeomanry of England'. The most revolutionary idea, the future cornerstone of the agricultural revolution, was to grow turnips and clover in place of the fallow period. In 1683 Worlidge noted that: 'Sheep fatten very well on turnips, which prove an excellent nourishment for them in hard winters, when fodder is scarce; for they will not only eat the greens, but feed on the roots in the ground, and scoop them hollow, even to the very skin.'

As turnips could be left in the ground for the first part of winter, they could be grazed or fed to cattle and sheep between December and February. Up until this time, farm animals were generally slaughtered before the onset of cold weather since there was no feed to keep them alive. By overwintering his animals, the farmer could increase the size of his herd. Animals on a good diet would produce more milk, more meat and richer manure.

Turnips and clover would also improve the soil more effectively than leaving the land fallow. Clover provides nitrogen from its roots and, when ploughed in as a green manure, it benefits the soil even further. Turnips are a vigorous groundclearing crop. Their broad leaves shade out weed growth. All in all, turnips and clover made a virtuous circle.

The idea was taken up by Charles 'Turnip' Townshend, secretary of state to George I. Although common mythology holds that he came up with this advance himself, in fact turnips were already growing on his family estate when he was a boy in the 1680s. However, he promoted the growing of turnips with such enthusiasm that he was ridiculed by the poet Alexander Pope, who remarked that he was 'particularly fond of that kind of rural improvement which arises from turnips; it was the favourite subject of his conversation.'

Lord Townshend is also credited with inventing the Norfolk Four Course, a four-year rotation in which turnips and clover replace the fallow period. He believed in the benefits of a mixed farm, following the old proverb that 'a full bullock yard and a full fold make a full granary'. He improved his land and transformed acres of previously uncultivable 'rush grown marshes' and poor sandy wastes into fertile fields. The Norfolk Four Course took a while to catch on, except in Norfolk itself. The writer Daniel Defoe, touring the countryside in 1722, noted that it was the part of England where 'the feeding and fattening of cattle, both sheep as well as black cattle, with turnips, was first practised.'

**The Norfolk Four Course & selective breeding**

It was during the eighteenth century that great advances were made in livestock breeding. Before this, farm animals were generally left to mate indiscriminately in the fields. Robert Bakewell, born in 1725 to a family of tenant farmers from Loughborough, Leicestershire, pioneered the technique of breeding 'in and in' by keeping the sexes separate except for arranged couplings, thus developing improved breeds. His large meaty, fine-fleeced, Leicester breeds were developed from native Lincolnshire sheep. So successful were they, that his stud rams were hired out to other breeders and were exported as far as the United States and Australia. His breeds eventually died out along with the fashion for fatty meat, but the English Leicester, kept for its fine wool, is a direct descendant.

From his farm in Leicestershire, Robert Bakewell produced champion breeds of sheep and cattle by developing a controlled approach to stockbreeding that is still the accepted practice.

Thomas Coke, Earl of Leicester – otherwise known as 'Coke of Norfolk' or the 'real hero of Norfolk agriculture' – tested out various novel ideas on his 12,000-hectare/30,000-acre estate. He converted and made productive soil so thin that one commentator imagined it had been ploughed by 'rabbits yoked to a pocket knife'. He tripled the size of his flocks to 2,400 by sowing the clover-like lucerne and drought-resistant cocksfoot grass for pasture. He experimented with crossbreeding and was said to have been the first to harness his oxen rather than using a yoke. He also tried 'floating' his water meadows for fresh grass in early spring. A thin film of river water was kept running over the slightly sloping grass, controlled by 'hatches', or

'Coke of Norfolk', who was interested in agricultural improvements, tripled the size of his flocks by sowing lucerne and cocksfoot grass for grazing. Here he is shown inspecting his sheep, in a painting in the style of Thomas Weaver.

sluice gates, and 'stops'. The water had to 'enter at a trot and leave at a gallop' – skilled work controlled by 'drowners' or watermen. The aim was to keep the pasture frost-free in winter to encourage a spurt of early growth for fodder in spring. Clearly an ingenious fellow, he was reported by the secretary to the Board of Agriculture, Arthur Young, to have saved a field full of turnips being decimated by black canker caterpillars, by releasing 400 ducks into the field to eat them.

Farmers began to graze their stock by day on the pasture and move the animals on to the bare arable land at night, to manure it. An economic alternative was stall-feeding, which allowed farmers to spread manure with precision on to the areas that needed it most.

Threshing by beating the grain with a flail was the lifeline that kept labourers going through the winter months, before the invention of the 'threshing machine'.

Experiments were also being made with a grain and grass rotation known as 'up-and-downhusbandry', 'ley' or 'convertible farming'. Land was ploughed up for arable for three to six years, then laid down to grass from selected seed for up to double that time, allowing it to be fertilized by grazing sheep. Although manure was without question the main fertilizer, other materials were considered: soot, hair, woollen rags, seaweed, fish and slaughterhouse waste, dried blood, malt dust, bone (lumps chopped up by hand, not ground down until the eighteenth century) and ash.

Oil cakes, made from the solid residue left from oil crops once the oil had been extracted, were trialled for feeding and fattening livestock. It was noted by John Mortimer, a Fellow of the Royal Society, that this innovation had not caught on. In his influential work *The Whole Art of Husbandry, or the Way of Managing and Improving of Land* (1707), he regretted that in Lincolnshire the farmers, having extracting the oil from coleseed (rape), mostly 'used the cakes to heat their ovens.' However, Mortimer took a dim view of growing potatoes as a farm crop – a suggestion proposed by John Forster in *England's Happiness Increased* (1664) as a way of helping the 'poorer sort' in years when the price of food was high. Mortimer described potatoes as 'good food for swine', which reflected the general opinion.

In 1676 John Worlidge published a further two books, containing interesting suggestions on how to profit from the land. *Vinetum Britannicum, or, A Treatise of Cider* pointed out the advantages of producing cider rather than wine in England, as it was better suited to the climate. *Apiarum, or, A Discourse of Bees* recommended growing fruit, not just for commercial reasons but, in advance of its time, for good health.

Incubators, in the form of boxes heated by a lamp or candles, were another idea of interest to eighteenth-century agriculturists. Silage, the high-moisture fodder, was proposed for feeding cattle and sheep in winter. Thought was also given to sowing seed in rows rather than broadcasting it by hand. Sir Hugh Plat, an agricultural writer and inventor from St Albans, was an early advocate of sowing corn by drilling, or 'setting'. He came across this idea by accident when a 'silly wench' sowed corn into the dibber holes intended for carrots.

In 1701 Jethro Tull invented his famous seed drill. This represented a long-awaited breakthrough (following various frustrated attempts by others) that would take much of the drudgery out of farming – but, compared to scattering seed by hand, it would also mean fewer jobs. Having had to abandon plans for a career in politics due to ill health, Tull, aged twenty-seven, was kicking his heels at his father's farm in Oxfordshire at the time. He began to experiment with growing sainfoin, a drought-resistant fodder plant in the pea family that improves dry soil. The seed was expensive and of poor quality, so Tull graded it and discovered, by trial and error, that sowing it to a precise depth and ensuring that it was covered 'exactly' produced the best crops.

From there it was a short step to the idea of making a mechanical means of sowing seed. The original model for his seed drill was built from the foot pedals of the local church organ. Tull describes how he 'at last pitched upon a groove, tongue and spring in the soundboard of an organ. With these, a little altered, and some parts of two other instruments, as foreign to the field as the organ is, added to them, I composed my machine.' The beauty of his invention was that it sowed seed in three equally spaced rows to the correct depth at regular intervals and in straight lines, thereby avoiding wastage in one simple operation.

In 1711, having moved to Prosperous Farm, near Hungerford, he decided to travel on the Continent to improve his health and also look into agricultural techniques. He was struck by the way the vineyards in the south of France were planted in parallel rows. This allowed for frequent ploughing to keep down weeds and 'stir' the soil, so that water and air could get to the roots. Inspired by this, he went on to invent a mechanical horse-drawn hoe, which weeded between the rows of crops, crumbling the soil as it went. It had a plough with blades set at an angle to pull up grass and weed roots. In 1731 he wrote *Horse Hoeing Husbandry*, setting out his discoveries.

**The thresher**    In 1784 the threshing machine was invented, which fifty years later was to bring on revolt in the countryside. The brainchild of Andrew Meikle, a Scottish millwright who was descended from 'a line of ingenious mechanics', the thresher could be powered by a watermill, windmill or horses. Later, steam was used. The sheaves were fed into a rotating drum that shook them up, letting the corn and the chaff drop through a grating before pushing the straw out. The chaff would be separated from the corn in a fanning mill operated with riddles, sieves and a flow of air.

The agricultural community at large was resistant to change from the old ways. Many of the revolutionary ideas did not take off for nearly a century. It was recorded that Queen Caroline, wife of George II, bought a copy of Tull's *Horse Hoeing Husbandry* and that the machines were discussed at court – but the farming population was not keen to make changes. Walter Blith, in *The English Improver Improved* (1649), had described the small farmers as 'mouldy old leavened husbandmen who themselves and their forefathers have been

An early horse-powered, hand-fed threshing machine. Machines like this were destroyed during the Swing Riots of 1830.

accustomed to such a course of husbandry as they will practise, and no other, their resolution is so fixed, no issues or events whatsoever shall change them.' However, by 1800 even the most diehard of arable farmers had succumbed to some form of mechanization, at least the threshing machine, at further cost to their labourers. It would become the symbol of their lost livings, as threshing in the old way with flails was the lifeline that had kept the men and their families ticking over through winter.

# 5. PARLIAMENTARY ENCLOSURES & THE FIRST ALLOTMENT MOVEMENT 1750–1850

'Inclosure came and trampled on the grave
Of labour's rights and left the poor a slave'
John Clare, 'The Mores' (1821–1824)

The eighteenth century saw the Hanoverian dynasty accede to the British throne and a shift in power from king to politicians. A disgruntled George II, who was crowned in 1727, remarked that 'Ministers are kings in this country.' Robert Walpole, the nation's first prime minister in all but name, was notoriously soon followed by William Pitt the Elder, who led the country through the Seven Years War of 1756–1763. He was dubbed the Great Commoner and was known for his brilliant oratory.

This was the Age of Enlightenment and the time of Pope, Swift, Defoe and Dr Johnson. The political figures of Georgian England were lampooned in the unsparing satirical cartoons of James Gillray and George Cruikshank, most of which were tolerated by the Establishment.

On 4 July 1776, America declared its independence. Thirteen years later the French Revolution and the subsequent Reign of Terror cast a long shadow of fear over Britain. The French peasant armies, known as the *sans-culottes* for their long trousers in place of silken knee-breeches, overran Belgium and declared war on the Netherlands. Bonaparte, then a young Corsican officer, was dispatched to Egypt to

The French Revolution and its aftermath aroused fears of insurrection that influenced the British élite for generations. Political cartoonist George Cruikshank here condemns the excesses of the Paris Commune of 1871, and by implication those seeking radical reforms in Britain.

attack British interests and was famously defeated at sea in 1805, in the Battle of Trafalgar. The Napoleonic Wars only finally ended in 1815, in the Battle of Waterloo under the Duke of Wellington.

In the late eighteenth century, life in Britain was changing at speed. Fortunes were to be made. Land was needed to feed the burgeoning population and keep up with advances in agriculture. But as vast tracts of the commons were enclosed, the peasants faced ruin. Many would lose their livelihood, their community, their home and, almost certainly, their customary and long-held right to grow food. With the French Revolution still fresh in their minds, and aware of the pressures weighing on the rural poor, the government of the day began to think of ways to improve their lot. Suggested solutions were many and varied, and even included the modern practice of a minimum wage. Ultimately, however, it was the idea of the provision of land for the poor that would be the most vigorously pursued.

Two million hectares/five million acres of land had been enclosed by 1845, equivalent to roughly one-third of the total agricultural land in England. By this time, the procedure used to obtain enclosure had evolved. During the Tudor period, interested parties generally reached private agreements that were recorded, for example, at the Court of Chancery. Where there were lots of conflicting interests, however, and agreement was difficult to obtain, a private Act of Parliament, though more expensive, was more efficient and watertight. This was a system whereby private individuals or groups could petition for benefits or powers which were of concern to local areas rather than the general public. Petitions to parliament were also frequently used in the nineteenth century for such matters as the building of roads, railways and canals.

From the 1750s, in the rush to enclose the 'common lands, wastes and open fields', enclosures were increasingly conducted as private Acts of Parliament. Some 1,500 private enclosure Acts took place before 1800. By 1845 the number of petitions had reached 3,500. To cut the red tape and save time, from 1801 the government brought in a series of legislation that provided a common framework for all enclosure petitions. In 1845, the General Enclosure Act finally removed the involvement of Parliament by handing over all responsibility to permanently appointed Enclosure Commissioners. From 1899, the Board of Agriculture (later the Ministry of Agriculture and Fisheries) took over this role.

## Parliamentary enclosures

The population of England, Scotland and Wales was 7.25 million in 1751. By the census of 1801, it had almost doubled. Thirteen years later it reached 16.5 million. The influential economist, Thomas Malthus, author of 'An Essay on the Principle of Population' (1798), claimed that food supplies were not keeping up with the rise in population – that whereas food production was increasing by 'arithmetical progression', the population was increasing by 'geometric progression'. Mass starvation was forecast.

New scientific methods and agricultural machinery gradually began to be adopted. More wasteland was brought into cultivation through reclamation. As a result, cereal farming almost doubled, keeping pace with the population explosion. Agriculture managed to supply 98 per cent of the British consumption of bread – still the staple food of the poor – until well into the nineteenth century.

This was a great achievement, but with it came devastating collateral damage to the agricultural labourers. They were brushed aside and barely considered. Many now had no land, no jobs, and neither the money or the education to represent themselves. Lord Lincoln, when introducing the General Enclosure Bill of 1845, pointed out the injustices of enclosure obtained by petition to Parliament:

**Neglect of the poor**

'In nineteen cases out of twenty, committees of this House, sitting on private bills, neglected the rights of the poor. I do not say that they willfully neglected those rights: far from it; but this I affirm, that they were neglected in consequence of the committees being permitted to remain in ignorance of the claims of the poor man, because by reason of his very poverty he is unable to come up to London to fee counsel, to produce witnesses, and to urge his claims before a committee of this House.'

**Making a petition**

A single signature was all that had been needed for the landowner to make a petition to Parliament in the early days.

Stephen Addington's 1767 work, *An Inquiry into the Reasons for and against Enclosing the Open Fields*, included the comment that 'the whole plan is generally settled between the solicitor and two or three principal proprietors without ever letting the rest of them into the secret till they are called upon to sign the petition.' Only after 1774 was the petitioner required to inform the parish of his plans by fixing a notice on the church door for three Sundays in August or September.

Once a petition had been accepted, permission would be granted for a bill to be introduced to the House of Commons. The bill would be heard twice before being referred to a committee of commissioners, who then considered the matter and drew up a report. The commissioners were generally peers, clergymen or gentlemen; also represented was the rising class of Parliamentarians who had profited from the Civil War and were characterized as the 'committee of landlords'. All were landowners, in other words, whose interests lay on the side of enclosure.

This offered an opportunity for unfair dealing that did not go unnoticed by Sir John Sinclair, economist and first president of the Board of Agriculture. He observed that usual practice was 'the appointment of one commissioner by the lord of the manor, of another by the tithe-owner and of a third by a major part in value of the proprietors'. Not until 1801 did the injustice of this arrangement dawn on Parliament, when a Standing Order was put in place to prevent the lord of the manor, his bailiff or steward, or any other proprietors concerned, from acting as commissioners for their own land.

While the committee was working on a private enclosure bill, objections could in principle be sent in. Incapable of doing this, and effectively excluded from the process, villagers expressed their opposition by rioting. They tore down fences and boundary hedges in their local parishes, filled in ditches and, on occasion, rebelled in such numbers that the military were called in to quell them. However, this had no effect on the wave of enclosures.

The enclosure acts largely put an end to the Church tithes being paid in kind to the parish church. Long since a source of disputes, from the eighteenth century tithes were generally paid in cash payments known as 'corn rents' or negotiated as allotments of land as part of individual enclosure agreements.

Once passed, the bill would go to the House of Lords to receive royal assent. The same commissioners who had been on the committee would then visit the estate and divide it as they saw fit. A share of the commons would go to the lord of the manor, another to the owners of tithes. Sometimes a small provision, an 'enclosure award' or 'allotment' (the origin of the term) would be made to the poorer members of the community. Arthur Young, secretary to the Board of Agriculture from 1793 to 1811, remarked that commissioners were invested with 'a despotic power known in no other branch of business in this free country'.

Enclosure changed the English countryside forever, most of all in the Midlands and the east of the country. Neat, uniform squares and rectangles replaced the wide, open fields with their patchwork of strips that had stretched as far as the eye could see. Hedges, which had to be planted within twelve months of an enclosure order, were often of hawthorn and were planted in staggered double rows 1.8–3 metres/6–10 feet wide to keep in stock and provide shade. They were one small blessing for the beleaguered peasant, as they offered wood, berries and nuts to the passer-by. Today, there is great interest in preserving and replacing hedges because of their value as wildlife habitats.

## Arthur Young and the land debate

The miserable plight of the farm labourer finally began to be raised in government circles and among the more philanthropic landowners. They began to think of allotting some land. A leading voice in the debate was Arthur Young. The son of a rector, he travelled in France just before the French Revolution and is possibly most renowned for his book *The Example of France: A Warning to Britain* (1793). While Young approved of enclosures for the advancement of agriculture, he became convinced that the way to help the struggling labourers was to give them back their traditional right to some land, and he put forward a number of revolutionary ideas on land distribution.

Laying out his proposals for allotments in *Observations on the Present State of the Wastelands of Great Britain* (1773), he suggested that the government buy all wasteland that came on to the market and sell it in lots of 8–12 hectares/20–30 acres to the poor. Families with eight or more children would be provided with a lot (or allotment) free of charge. In 1784 Young founded the *Annals of Agriculture*, a monthly publication that carried on a lively discourse for thirty-two years. Contributors included the good and the great. George III provided articles under the pseudonym Ralph Robinson.

In 1793 Young was appointed to the newly established Board of Agriculture under Sir John Sinclair. The Board came up with three rather more moderate suggestions for a General Enclosure Bill

# ENCLOSURES IN ENGLAND

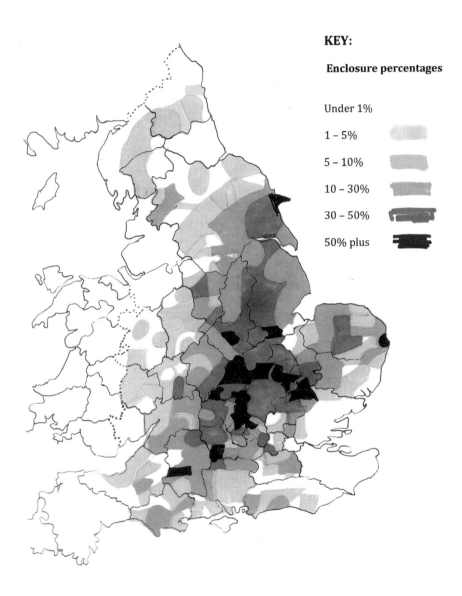

**KEY:**

**Enclosure percentages**

Under 1%

1 – 5%

5 – 10%

10 – 30%

30 – 50%

50% plus

The distribution of enclosures 1750–1850, showing that the areas worst hit were the Midlands, the South-West and South-East.

between 1795 and 1800. They recommended that a portion of the wasteland should be set aside for allotments on a permanent basis and run by the lord of the manor, the vicar or rector, the church wardens or the overseers. Any labourer over twenty-one with settlement in the parish would be able to take on an allotment, rent-free, for fifty years. In return, they would build a cottage and fence the land. After this, they could renew the lease at a reasonable rent, for a further twenty-one years. Half the rent would go to the landowner and the other half to the poor rates. People who had previously had the right to gather firewood would be provided with fuel allotments.

These proposed bills met with so much opposition that the Board of Agriculture was obliged to try a completely different tack. The Enclosure Consolidation Bill of 1801, while recommending that provision should be made for the smallest owners, smoothed the way for further enclosures and included none of Young's ideas. In fury and frustration, Young brought out a paper on the very eve of the hearing, entitled 'An Inquiry into the Propriety of Applying Wastes to the Better Maintenance and Support of the Poor'. He was only permitted to publish it on condition that it was made crystal clear that it was written without the backing or approval of the Board of Agriculture or of its new president, Lord Carrington.

Young wrote: 'To pass Acts beneficial to every other class in the state and hurtful to the lowest class only, when the smallest alteration would prevent it, is a conduct against which reason, justice and humanity equally plead.' He suggested that half a million families should be provided with allotments and cottages. The parishes could set this up by borrowing money from the government and paying it back through funds collected as rates. Should a family fail to pay the rates, the cottage and land would revert to the parish. This idea was met with derision and the bill passed into law.

In 1836 a General Enclosure Bill was passed which allowed for the enclosure of common fields without sanction by Parliament, as long as a majority of two-thirds of the parties involved were in agreement. Central commissioners were appointed to ensure that justice was done. No provision was made for allotments. Arthur

Young, who died in 1820, would have been disappointed; but he had no regrets about his last-minute paper in 1801, as he made clear in his autobiography: 'Thank God I wrote it, for though it never had the smallest effect except in exciting opposition and ridicule, it will, I trust, remain a proof of what ought to have been done; and had it been executed, would have diffused more comfort among the poor than any proposition that was ever made.'

Young was not alone in taking this stand. Others were speaking out. The agricultural writer and Norfolk land agent, William Marshall, remarked on the self-seeking attitude of the landowners. They were not 'pressing forward with offerings and sacrifices to relieve the present distresses of the country', but instead were 'searching for vantage ground to aid them in the scramble'.

Thomas Stone recommended in *Suggestions* **Those in favour** *for Rendering the Inclosure of Common Fields and Waste Lands a Source of Population and Riches* (1787) that following an enclosure, farms should be made available to labourers in varying sizes from £40 to £200 a year.

As early as 1775, Nathaniel Kent, estate agent and land valuer, one time bailiff to George III's estate at Windsor, expressed concern in *Hints to Gentlemen of Landed Property* about the practice of throwing small farms together, as it raised the cost of living for the workers. Whereas labourers could once buy milk, butter and other provisions in every parish, 'since small farms have decreased in number, no such articles are to be had; for the great farmers have no idea of retailing such small commodities, and those who do retail them, carry them all to towns.' He suggested that farmers should reduce the size of their farms and raise wages. Over the previous fifty years the price of provisions had increased by 60 per cent while wages had risen by only 25 per cent. Other commentators encouraged the impoverished to eat more

William Pitt the Younger, prime minister at the age of 24 in 1783, complained that the poor had 'unfounded prejudices against coarse brown bread'.

A keen reason given for providing allotments was to keep the labourer occupied, grateful and sober. Above all, it was seen as a way to reduce the burdensome poor rates.

economically. William Pitt the Younger accused the poor of having 'groundless prejudices' against coarse brown bread.

Opinions on the merits of allotments varied. Some believed that land would benefit the poor by providing them with a better diet, better health and something to strive for – a source of hope and a degree of independence. Some believed it would produce better and more grateful workers or servants. Others said that access to land would train the next generation in agricultural skills, or that labourers would be more likely to stay rather than seek work in the towns, or

Those against allocations of land supposed that the poor would be too tired to look after it properly, or spend any profits from the sale of produce in the alehouse – or, worse still, get above their station.

indeed that it would allow employers to stabilize or even reduce wages. A prime consideration was that allocations of land would reduce the burden of the poor rates.

Keeping the poor out of the alehouse, making them more industrious and improving their morals were important objectives to those in favour of allotments. A correspondent to the *Annals of Agriculture* wrote in 1796 that 'A few roods of land, at a fair rent, would do a labourer as much good as wages almost doubled; there would not, then, be an idle hand in his family; and the man himself would often go to work in his root yard, instead of going to the alehouse.' Arthur Young, in his 1801 paper, painted a convincing picture of the poor worn down by a lack of prospects, who might indeed ask: 'If I am diligent, shall I have leave to build a cottage? If I am sober, shall I have land for a cow? If I am frugal, shall I have half an acre of potatoes?

You offer no motives; you have nothing but a parish officer and a workhouse! Bring me another pot.'

**Those against**
Counter arguments included the view that labourers did not cultivate the land well, that they would be too exhausted after a day's work to do any more, or that they would neglect their work in favour of their own land. Some believed that if they had enough land to feed their families, they would not want to work at all. A certain Mr Billingsley, in a report on Somerset for the Board of Agriculture in 1794, considered that 'The possession of a cow or two with a hog, and a few geese, naturally exalts the peasant in his own conception, above his brethren ... In sauntering after his cattle he acquires a habit of indolence ... and at length the sale of a half-fed calf, or hog, furnishes the means of adding intemperance to idleness.'

Another correspondent took the view that, judging by past experience, commoners looking after 'a few rotten sheep, a skeleton of a cow or a mangy horse' lost more than 'they might have gained by their day's work, and acquired habits of idleness and dissipation and a dislike to honest labour, which has rendered them the riotous and lawless set of men which they have now shown themselves to be.' Farmers were against the labourers getting 'too saucy' and above themselves, so they would 'breed' more children and demand higher wages. A report in the Poor Law Commission of 1834 found evidence that farmers' attitudes were an obstacle in the prevention of pauperism, noting: 'They prefer that the labourers should be slaves; they object to their having gardens, saying, *The more they work for themselves, the less they work for us.*'

## Leading by kindness – the first Allotment Movement

Despite the staunch opposition from some quarters, those convinced of the need for allotments gave thought to the different ways that land could be provided to the labourer. A letter to the Board of Agriculture from the Earl of Winchilsea in 1796 presented a range of possibilities. The cheapest form of land provision was the potato ground, usually allocated on areas of land not in use – wastes, fallows, verges or corners of fields that could easily

**Potato grounds**

be turned over for a crop of potatoes. They were let on a temporary basis, so were commitment-free for the landowners and were an easy way to help hungry workers in times of hardship. They brought an added advantage to the farmer: their wasteland would be dug over, and – as potatoes are a good clearing crop – a following crop of corn would benefit. An article from Cheshire published in the *Annals of Agriculture* in 1800 makes this point in support of the scheme: 'As no ready money passes, the temptation of spending a part of the profit in the alehouse is avoided: the farmer is also well repaid for his land by sharing the produce, together with the prospect of an abundant succeeding crop.'

'Home colonization', the most expensive scheme, was aimed at halting the rise in emigration. It would lift the labourer out of poor relief by providing him with a piece of land and possibly a cottage. He would no longer be a hired labourer but an independent small farmer or yeoman. This was along the same lines as Arthur Young's 1773 proposal to break up large farms or spare land into small shares. A more moderate suggestion was to provide up to 2 hectares/5 acres of arable fields per head.

**Home colonization**

The idea of the garden attached to the cottage was the most highly favoured. The labourer would want to get home to his cottage and so would be out of the way of temptation. It would encourage domesticity and improve family life. It would give the landowner a carrot, but also a stick. Any misdemeanour, any offence against the law or an application for poor relief, could result in confiscation of the land.

**A cott and a cow**

Many saw the advantages of giving workers a cow for dairy products, including milk for their children. Some argued that if the workers had milk to drink they might forego their indulgent taste for tea and beer – a stubborn habit of which they disapproved. Milk was also useful for fattening pigs. One writer in the *Annals of Agriculture* spotted an unforeseen advantage. He suggested that the poor should resort to stables for warmth, as was the practice in the Duchy of Milan. Fewer would suffer death from want of a fire in winter, he argued, and it would be a cheap way of helping them, because of the warmth given out by the bodies of the cattle. However, the disincentive to providing a cow was the cost involved, which included the provision of summer pasture, land for hay or winter fodder and a cowshed. It was cheaper for farmers simply to 'let' one of their own cows for milking by their labourers.

In 1796, the Society for Bettering the Condition and Increasing the Comforts of the Poor (SBCP) was set up. It marked a milestone in the history of British welfare provision and, along with the debate surrounding the provision of land, set off the first Allotment Movement. The society was founded by the antislavery campaigner, William Wilberforce, the Bishop of Durham and philanthropist Thomas Bernard. The members of the society were drawn from the gentry and included bishops, nobles and George III. This ensured influence at the highest level. Many SBCP members were also involved with the Board of Agriculture and the Royal Institute. The three organizations had one goal in common: to improve agriculture and help the rural poor following the food shortages of the revolutionary and continuing Napoleonic Wars with France.

The Revd Stephen Demainbray, author of *The Poor Man's Best Friend* (1831) and chaplain to George III, in 1809 persuaded the king to give over some land in perpetuity at Great Somerford, in Wiltshire, creating what could arguably be seen as the first allotments. Sir Thomas Estcourt, of Shipton Moyne in Gloucestershire, was another pioneer. Writing in a SBCP report in 1800, he described the nearby village of Long Newnton, where 140 poor people, mostly labourers, were in debt despite receiving poor relief. As the landowner, he gave each cottager the opportunity of renting a piece of land no larger than 0.6 hectares/1.5 acres, depending on the size of their family. They were loaned £44 to pay off their debts. Applying for poor relief was not permitted and a quarter of the land had to be planted with potatoes. They were allotted a third of the land in the first year and the rest in equal amounts over the following two years. From that day, Estcourt reported, none applied for poor relief and all paid off their debts promptly. The farmers also admitted to him that 'they never had their work better done, their servants more able, willing, civil, and sober, and that their property was never so free from depredation as at present.' Estcourt extended the scheme by attaching 0.2 hectares/0.5 acres to each cottage, placed under the supervision of the church wardens and overseers, and providing 3.2 hectares/8 acres for allotments. The results were encouraging, with 'every man looking forward to becoming a man of property'.

The Earl of Egremont, another active member on the Board of Agriculture, provided his estate workers with 1.2 hectares/3 acres each. His steward noted that a warm cottage and a plot of land made the labourers 'the most contented of workers'. Lord Winchilsea, also a board member, was the proprietor of four parishes in Rutland. His eighty cottagers owned 174 cows between them and most owned a pig. A third of them owned their land, while others had the use of some land in addition to their cottage and garden. Winchilsea attempted an experiment: he decided to provide them with some common grazing for cattle. The result was that the cottagers, described as 'most steady and trusty', paid their rents more punctually than any other tenants on the estate.

The first allotments were mostly in Wiltshire and Gloucestershire. There were a few sites around the south of England, as well as in the Midlands and East Anglia – possibly one hundred across the whole country. If nothing else, a precedent had been established and allotments proven to work. Thomas Bernard, one of the founders of the SBCP, writing in the journal of 1805, expressed the opinion that the only way to improve the conditions of the poor was to lay the foundation for an improvement in their 'moral and religious character'. The Poor Law, he pointed out, had attempted to force them to be industrious without success for 200 years. Now it was time to 'lead by kindness'.

# 6. WILLIAM COBBETT & THE SWING RIOTS OF 1830

'The grand rousing will come from the fellows
with hobnails on their shoes.'
William Cobbett, *Rural Rides* (1830)

A mong the heroes who light up the dark history of allotments is
William Cobbett, champion of the labouring poor. Self-taught
and from a humble farming background himself, he was to write
some 25 million words on subjects as diverse as English grammar
and the Protestant Reformation. His *Cottage Economy* (1822), which
dispensed practical advice on such matters as brewing beer and
fattening hogs, was aimed to help the labourers to a greater degree
of independence.

Cobbett is most celebrated as a high-profile radical political
commentator and brilliant literary journalist. His publication, the
*Political Register,* which ran into eighty-nine volumes between 1802
and 1835, campaigned tirelessly to improve the lot of the labourer.
His programme of 'radical husbandry' went further, aiming to
undermine the tax collector, the cash market and the accumulation of
capital, resulting in the redistribution of wealth. He urged for reform
of the Corn Laws, universal suffrage and annual parliaments. His was
a lone voice warning of the danger of a violent uprising if action was
not taken to prevent it.

## Rustic harangues

Cobbett was born in Farnham, Surrey, in 1763. In his youth he graduated from bird-scaring as a farm lad, to the 'honour of joining in the reapers in harvest, driving team and holding plough'. At the age of twenty-one, he joined the army and was sent to New Brunswick in Canada, where he rose to the rank of sergeant major and studied English and French in his spare time.

Following his return to England and military discharge in 1791, Cobbett published *The Soldier's Friend,* exposing the harsh conditions and corruption within the military. Repercussions from this led to his hasty departure to republican France with his new bride, Nancy Anne Reid. After a few months, the couple moved on to America. Here, writing under the pseudonym Peter Porcupine, Cobbett condemned the French Revolution. In *A Bone to Gnaw for the Democrats* (1795), he attacked the republican element that was predicting revolution in England. This essay was so popular that it ran to three reprints in the space of three months. The torrent of other pamphlets he produced railing against any prospect of a Franco-American alliance against Britain caught the attention of William Pitt the Younger and his Tory ministers, who invited Cobbett to dine with them on his return to Britain in 1800. Over the years, however, Cobbett's right-wing, anti-republican tendencies gave way to sympathy for the Jacobin cause and support for parliamentary reform. In time, he embraced the ideals of tolerance and equality advocated by the Levellers of the seventeenth century.

In 1802 Cobbett founded a radical weekly newspaper, the *Political Register,* which gives a fascinating insight into his social and political views and was published, against all odds, until his death in 1835. A leading article he wrote in 1810 exposed the flogging of soldiers, landing him in Newgate prison for two years. However, he had sympathizers in high places. When he was released, Sir Francis Burdett, the reformer and advocate of popular rights, gave a dinner for him with 600 guests. Cobbett also had a following among the less affluent: his *Political Register* became one of the main journals read by the working class, reaching a circulation of over 40,000 after

**Cobbett's Political Register**

Cobbett found a way to produce a cheaper version. By selling the publication in broadsheet form he avoided the prohibitive tax on newspapers. This had reached 4d a copy by 1815 and was in effect an attempt by the government to restrict their circulation and repress free speech.

In parallel with his writing, Cobbett continued his farming activities throughout his life. In 1805 he had bought a farm in Hampshire, where he became increasingly interested and involved in rural life. In 1823 he started to transform a 'rough and sour meadow' of 1.6 hectares/4 acres in Kensington into a nursery farm where there stood 'more than a million of seedling forest trees and shrubs and three thousand young apple trees'. In 1826 he leased Barn Elm, 'a walled in plot' in open countryside south of the Thames. It was here, in his later years, that he experimented widely with unusual farm crops and methods. He tried Indian corn, Italian straw (with the

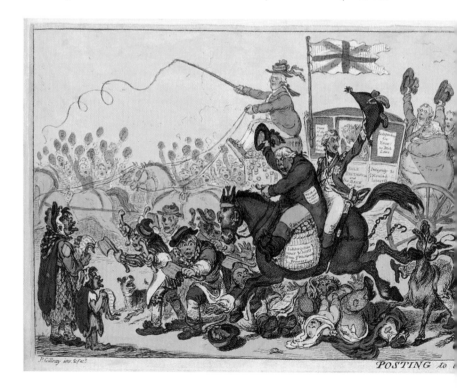

aim of reviving English straw-plaiting as a source of winter work for labourers) and merino sheep.

When back from America, it had struck Cobbett that many farmers were struggling to make ends meet and were 'obliged to work very hard'. He witnessed the worsening state of poverty among the labourers compared to the rural England of his youth, commenting in the *Political Register* during 1805: 'The *clock* was gone; the *brass kettle* was gone; the *pewter dishes* were gone ... the *feather bed* was gone; the *Sunday-coat* was gone! All was gone! How miserable, how deplorable, how changed that labourer's dwelling, which I, only twenty years

William Cobbett intended to stand for Parliament in 1806 but was persuaded not to. In this James Gillray sketch entitled *Posting to the Election*, Cobbett can be seen on the far right, banging a drum with a rolled-up copy of his *Political Register* in support of Sir Francis Burdett.

— *a Scene on the Road to Brentford. Nov.ʳ 1806* —

before, had seen so neat and so happy!' He remarked on how much land had become enclosed, how prosperous farmers cared nothing for their workers, and how the landed gentry and the yeoman got rich while workers starved. It became his mission to help farm labourers by representing their interests, drawing attention to their plight and giving voice to their needs.

***Rural Rides***     Although Cobbett's first loyalty was to the 'chopsticks' of his home patch, men he described as the 'very best and most virtuous of all mankind', he decided to travel further afield to find out for himself what was going on in farming circles in surrounding counties, and to see what he could do to help the labourers. In 1821 he began his celebrated tour of southern England on horseback. His mission was to get a first-hand view of the reality of rural life, to find the truth, to talk to the labourers in the fields, meet the farmers at home or eat with them in their 'own places of resort'. On his travels he observed 'enclosures without end', 'villages wasting away', 'shocking decay' and 'great dilapidation'. The thoughts he recorded at the end of each day were published as a series of articles in the *Political Register*, and later in book form as *Rural Rides*, which is still in print and much enjoyed today.

During his tour, he made a point of visiting Farmers' Meetings to express his views. These were attended by the larger landowners and the wealthier farmers who rode with the Yeoman Cavalry. The meetings were usually only open to freeholders, so Cobbett had to wangle his way in, often under false pretences, and speak for the labourers who were not admitted. His long harangues, lasting an hour or two, were often met with sullen silence or sour looks. This is not surprising as the farmers' main objective in these meetings was to petition for a tightening up of the Corn Laws. They had slackened by the 1820s, bringing their profits down.

He prevailed upon his unwilling audience to put forward the interests of the labourers and small farmers – to make a countryman's alliance and petition Parliament for reduced taxes, increased suffrage to give the labourers a voice, and also reform of the Poor Law, so that they were no longer treated as 'beasts of burden'. He proclaimed that the landowner's profits came off the back of the workers, and that he would never reduce the wages of his own labourers under any circumstances – but would share to the last, even if on 'the verge of ruin'.

While Cobbett's main objectives were political and not directly concerned with land or allotments, his voice resounded throughout society on the scandal of the way the country poor were treated. There is an interesting description in *Rural Rides* of what could be described as an early allotment, although Cobbett perceived it as a welcome return of the commons. When in Tetbury, Gloucestershire, he saw a woman digging some potatoes in a field that appeared to be 'laid out in strips'. To his delight he discovered that the farmer let out these strips to labouring people. He noted that the farmer paid the taxes, repaired the fences, that the land was in good heart and rent was fair enough. He saw it as 'a little step towards a *coming back* of the ancient small *life* and *lease* holds and *common-fields*!' He rued the day when enclosures had shut the labourers out of '*all share* in the land'.

Cobbett had a fine line in rhetoric. He scorned the newly rich 'who had risen recently from the dunghill', the greedy 'bull dog farmers' and the gentry, whom he referred to as 'these mean, these cruel, these cowardly, these carrion, these dastardly reptiles'. He railed in fury about two men found lying dead under a hedgerow one winter with nothing but 'sour sorrel in their bellies'.

The English farm labourer was now Europe's pauper. The French peasants, once considerably worse off, were now the more fortunate because they still had access to land. In the French Revolution that finally freed them from feudalism – more than 200 years after its disappearance from Britain – all feudal dues on agricultural land were abolished without compensation and the title deeds destroyed. In the summer of 1830, there was further revolutionary unrest in Europe. Charles X of France was ousted in favour of Louis Philippe, the 'Citizen King'. That August, Belgium freed itself from Dutch control, and in November there was an uprising in Poland. Although most labourers at this time were illiterate, news such as this still reached their ears. Cheap newspapers and news-sheets, like Cobbett's

*Political Register* and others, including the *Weekly Dispatch* and the *Sunday Times,* would have been discussed in the beer-houses and market squares.

In Britain, social and economic pressures were building to a crisis. Unemployment was rife, exacerbated by the addition of a quarter of a million soldiers and sailors demobilized in 1815, at the end of the Napoleonic Wars. That same year the Tory government under Lord Liverpool had passed a Corn Law, to protect the home market and bigger farms by restricting the import of foreign corn. The influential political economist, Thomas Malthus, author of 'An Essay on the Principle of Population' (1798), took the view that flooding the country with cheap imported corn would only serve to reduce the labourer's wages. Unfortunately, the side effect of the law was to drive up the price of bread, with serious consequences for the poor, especially those without access to land. Cobbett pointed out that the 'agricultural-asses' – as he liked to call the land-owning agriculturists – had enjoyed high prices for their wheat through the boom years of the Napoleonic Wars, but were wrong to expect their 'extravagant gains' to continue in peacetime.

These hardships were compounded by other difficulties facing the rural population. Machinery – particularly the threshing machine – was reducing opportunities for winter work. Hiring fairs were now few, and farm servants were becoming a thing of the past. Wages were topped up to the barest subsistence levels according to the price of bread under the Speenhamland System (see page 62), giving labourers no more than needed to prevent starvation. The 1662 Settlement Act (see page 59) continued to tie people to their village of origin, preventing their search for work, and imprisoned paupers in the hated workhouses. There was no hope of betterment. There were no prospects.

Revolution was in the air. Bread or Blood riots, sometimes comprised both of hungry town and country workers, erupted spasmodically. One such disturbance, fuelled by beer, started at the Globe Inn at Littleport, Cambridgeshire, in 1816. Unemployed workers, furious at the cost of bread, stormed the town's wealthier areas, demanding cash and food, threatening violence, causing damage and stealing money. Things got further out of hand the next day, with larger numbers joining at Ely. Magistrates tried to diffuse the riots by ordering poor relief and laying down a minimum wage. When this failed to quell the mob, dragoons rounded them up in a gun battle. Some hid in the fens for weeks. A bolter was shot dead. Five unfortunates were hanged and the remaining nineteen transported to Botany Bay for seven years.

Then came the poor harvest of 1829, which had been so bad that it was not brought in until after the snows in October. Something had to give. Cobbett had been warning farmers of an impending uprising if they did nothing to help their workers. He implored them to change their ways and repeated ominous comments such as 'better be a dog than a farmer next winter'. He predicted that the peasants would not 'live on damned potatoes while the barns are full of corn, the downs covered with sheep, and the yards full of hogs created by their labours'. It was to no avail. Frustrated, Cobbett joined the rioters to witness and advise as fires burned in Kent and Sussex.

## The Swing Riots

In June 1830 a haystack was set alight at Orpington, in Kent. Over the following months rick-torching became so common in Kent that *The Times* said there was 'scarcely a night without some farmer having a corn stack or barn set fire to'. On 29 August the first threshing machine was destroyed, at Lower Hardres, near Canterbury. The next day another was wrecked at a farm near Hythe, not far from Folkestone. By mid-September eleven more had been targeted in the Canterbury area. Two weeks later the number had escalated to around one hundred. The destruction of threshing machines symbolized the loss of vital winter work from harvest time through to May, and was unique to the Swing Riots.

By October, *The Times* was reporting on the emergence of 'an organized system of stack burning and machine breaking'. Mobs of some 200 to 300 men armed with bludgeons and crowbars were marching, smashing up threshing machines and making their

SWING!
taken from the Life.
Dedicated to Messᵣ Cobbett. Carlisle. & Cᵒ

Cartoon of Captain Swing, with a rick burning to one side, a noose on the other, and Cobbett's *Political Register* in his pocket.

demands in broad daylight. Rick-burning spread into Surrey. Gangs called on houses asking for money, food and beer. Threatening notes would be left for the landowner or farmer, signed by the mythical Captain Swing. A typical message read: 'This is to advise you and the like of you ... to make your wills. Ye have been the blackguard enemies of the people on all occasions, ye have not yet done as ye ought.'

**Captain Swing**

A series of 'wage meetings' and 'tumultuous assemblies' began to take place. Demands were made for better pay: a day rate of 2/3d (two shillings and threepence) in winter and 2/6d in summer for a married man. There were parts of the country where wages were only 1/– a day, with paupers on half that amount. In Kent, seat of the revolts, wages were rarely more than 10/– a week. The average wage throughout the Swing counties was 8/4d a week, against which the rioters' demands represented a rise of 180 per cent.

**Tumultuous assemblies**

In return for higher wages, the rioters offered to help farmers by intimidating the church wardens into dropping the Church tithes. This they did with some success, often by arriving in force at the moment a tithe audit was due to be carried out. The smaller farmers, in whose interests it was to reduce tithes and taxes, sometimes even joined with the rioters to petition Parliament. There were many reports of collusion: suspicions that 'the farmers were at the bottom of it' and accusations that they were 'urging them to excesses'. It certainly appeared that the farmers were putting up little resistance. Reporting on the Swing Riots in November, *The Times* noted how they were not foolish enough to refuse requests that, after all, were 'not unreasonable in themselves' – especially as those demands had been put to them by '300 or 400 men after a barn or two had been fired and each farmer had an incendiary letter addressed to him in his pocket.' The *Brighton Herald* commented on the painful dilemma faced by the middle class of farmers, 'pressed on the one hand by their starving labourers, and on the other by the landlords and clergy'; and how they might feel 'compelled to make common cause with the former, whom they must consider as fellow sufferers, while the latter they must look upon as exactors and oppressors.'

**The farmer's view**

A letter to Sir Robert Peel, then serving as home secretary, expresses the viewpoint of a group of farmers and tradesmen from the area around Battle, East Sussex, who were told by local magistrates to raise the wages of labourers and relief for paupers. This they had done, they said, 'on a scale which we positively cannot continue for any length of time without bringing us all to one common ruin, and

Sir Robert Peel, home secretary under the Duke of Wellington.

which we have done to prevent our property from being destroyed by incendiaries.' They continue: 'We therefore implore His Majesty's government, if they value the existence of a middle class of society, to take off all taxes which press upon the industrious classes, otherwise there will be but two classes, the one most miserably poor and the other most extremely rich.'

The Swing Riots had some support among the higher social orders. In Kent, the Earl of Guildford, either through sympathy for the rioters or to avoid trouble, told his tenants not to use the threshing machines. Lord Northwick, in Worcestershire, sent his bailiff to break up a machine when his tenant refused to do so. A Justice of the Peace from Marlborough, Wiltshire, observed that 'the greatest number of the threshing machines destroyed have been put out for the purpose by the owners themselves.'

As the riots spread westwards, they became larger, more organized and more political. In Sussex there were a series of arson attacks on the overseers of the poor. These began with a fire at the house of an overseer in Battle; and then at Brede, nearby, where the despised incumbent was wheeled out of town in the parish cart escorted by 500 jeering labourers. This tactic was copied in other towns and villages. 'Where disorder has occurred,' reported *The Times* on 17 November, 'it has arisen from dislike of some obnoxious clergyman, or tithe man, or assistant overseer, who has been trundled out of the parish in a wheelbarrow, or drawn in triumph in a load of ballast by a dozen old women.'

Arson & the parish cart

Despite the violence, *The Times* commented on the admirable conduct of the peasantry, whose 'proceedings have been managed with astonishing coolness and regularity'. When farmers were invited to meet with a deputation of rioters, the written statement produced for the farmers to sign was usually 'well drawn up' and the spokesman, 'sometimes a Dissenting or Methodist teacher, fulfils his office with great propriety and temper'.

The Sussex villages of Arundel, Bersted, Bognor, Felpham and Yapton combined forces to march from one farm to the next, leaving a trail of smashed threshing machines and gathering more men as they went. One thousand labourers met with Justices of the Peace and farmers at Chichester, where they got their terms agreed. Within days of rebellion breaking out in Sussex, the riots peaked in Berkshire, Wiltshire and Hampshire.

The Duke of Buckingham wrote from the village of Avington, near Winchester, that 'this part of the country is wholly in the hands of the rebels ... 1,500 rioters are to assemble tomorrow morning and will attack any farmhouses where there are threshing machines.' At two other Hampshire villages, Selborne and Headley, a mob turned out the workhouses, pulled down the roofs and set fire to the furniture. The Headley workmaster later recorded that there was 'not a room left entire', other than the sick ward full of 'old paupers' and the children's ward, which had not been touched.

Emboldened by their successes, the rioters intensified their campaign of arson and destruction, which now included ploughs and other types of machinery. At Petersfield, in Hampshire, a mob 1,000 strong was observed passing through, destroying machines as they went.

**Hunted like game or cattle** Landowners responded by enrolling old soldiers, servants, loyal labourers, villagers and tenants to form their own local armies. The Duke of Wellington, who was prime minister through the early part of the riots, boasted that he had hunted down the Hampshire mobs 'like game or cattle'. Armed with 'horsewhips, pistols, fowling pieces and what they could get', his militia were sent out to disperse, destroy or round up the troublemakers. It was astonishing, the duke remarked later, 'how soon the country was tranquilized'. The Duke of Richmond assembled a constabulary force that was sent out pre-emptively to where trouble was anticipated. This strategy became known as the Sussex Plan and was widely adopted.

**Lenient magistrates** The first seven prisoners on trial for machine-breaking in Kent were given a mere three days of imprisonment and a warning. A Norfolk magistrate recommended 'a general disuse of the threshing machines as a friendly concession', while a Dorset magistrate suggested that anyone who refused to break up their threshing machines should only receive half the insured value of their corn in case of arson. Other magistrates expressed their approval of the new wage rates. However, the government was concerned about these signs of sympathy and Lord Melbourne, the new Whig home secretary, issued a rebuke. He argued that threshing machines were entitled to as much protection from the law as any other piece of property.

In response to this, one correspondent asked rhetorically: 'Can any excuse be offered for men who are so deaf to humanity and blind to their own permanent interest as to substitute horse power for

The Duke of Wellington, prime minister at the start of the Swing Riots, claimed to have run down the Hampshire mobs 'like game or cattle'.

manual labour and leave the population born on the soil, to subsist on a miserable pittance in idleness or unproductively employed on the roads?'

The riots had caught the government unprepared, partly because the Yeomanry Cavalry had been disbanded at the end of the Napoleonic Wars and the regular army reduced. Armed forces were now needed in order to crush resistance on home soil. Special constables were signed up. The Yeomanry Cavalry was mobilized in Wiltshire and every remaining cavalry soldier available was rounded up. The Chelsea Pensioners were pulled out of retirement and contingents of Dragoon Guards were established in Kent and West Sussex.

The rioters knew their limits. The Swing Riots petered out as suddenly as they had begun. By December 1830, nearly 2,000 people had been arrested. Convinced that the magistrates were too lenient, Lord Melbourne appointed Special Commissions to try the rioters. The commissioners did not sit in Kent or Sussex, where proceedings had begun, but in the towns of Winchester, Reading, Salisbury, Dorchester and Aylesbury.

**Capital punishment**

The stakes were high since destroying barns or buildings, extorting money by threatening means or forming part of a riotous crowd leading to extortion, violence or assault, were all capital offences – as was breaking machinery, except threshing machines, which carried the lesser penalty of transportation. Over four weeks the commission tried 894 cases. Although more than 300 of these were dismissed without charge, the remainder were less fortunate: 227 were initially sentenced to death, an almost equal number were sent to prison and a handful faced transportation. However, the death sentences were later commuted to long terms of transportation in all but eleven cases.

There was an immediate public outcry in response to the harsh sentences. Within thirty-six hours, a plea to reprieve the eleven doomed men arrived at Reading. It was signed by 1,500 people. A petition to the king from residents of Shaftesbury pointed out that 'in no instance … had it been the object of the distressed peasantry to shed the blood of their supposed oppressors.' The only death that had occurred during the riots had been that of a luckless rioter shot by a member of the Wiltshire Yeomanry in Tisbury. Although a motion for a general pardon was dismissed out of hand in the House of Commons, eight of the eleven were spared as a result of the entreaties received on their behalf. The total number of executions following the Swing Riots eventually numbered nineteen; more than 400 offenders were transported and around 600 were imprisoned.

Court records show that the rioters were predominantly farm

labourers. Most of these were ploughmen, but 'navigators' (navvies, or road labourers), stone-breakers and well-diggers had also participated, as had paupers and those out of work. Wheelwrights, sawyers, carpenters and blacksmiths, with the skills to dismantle threshing machines, had taken a key role. Seven women were prosecuted and a few farmers also went on trial, some with scores to settle with the local parson or squire. Certain offenders had no personal reason to begrudge the threshing machine (as magistrates would point out acidly) – including clockmakers and thatchers. The leaders of the uprising were the more educated shopkeepers and craftsmen, as well as various dissidents. The rioters were generally of good character, and most were married men in their thirties. Two-thirds had no criminal record and of the others, most had been guilty only of minor crimes such as poaching or petty theft. Public pressure led to the majority of Swing Riot convicts being freed over the next few years.

In July 1831, William Cobbett was tried for libel due to an **Cobbett's** article entitled 'Rural War' that had appeared in his journal, **libel case** the *Political Register*. It expressed his support for the Swing Riots and discussed how the inequalities of society could be remedied by parliamentary reform, but Cobbett denied the government's claim that it had incited rural labourers to acts of violence. In a typically bold stroke, he subpoena'd six members of the cabinet, including the prime minister Earl Grey and Lord Melbourne. Having conducted his own defence, he succeeded in discrediting the prosecution and was acquitted, to the great embarrassment of the government.

Following the Great Reform Act the year after, Cobbett's long-held dream of becoming an MP was finally fulfilled in 1833, when he was elected at the age of seventy to represent Oldham. Although as critical as ever, he was proud of this success, and said he would call his autobiography 'The Progress of a Ploughboy to a Seat in Parliament'.

# 7. LAND, THE LABOURERS' FRIEND & THE SECOND ALLOTMENT MOVEMENT 1832–1914

> 'Land, land: that was what we were all
> thinking about and talking about, and the idea
> of an Allotment Act was in the air.'
> *Joseph Arch (1881)*

It was on the third attempt, following riots and disturbances, resignations and ministerial pressure on William IV, that the Great Reform Act had finally become law in 1832. Steered through by Earl Grey and an enlightened Whig Cabinet, it increased the franchise from 500,000 to 813,000, and was the first step towards real change in the balance of power between civilians and the state. It also tackled the question of rotten boroughs and created new seats for the great northern industrial cities. It had been a close call, however. Full-blooded revolt had seemed a real possibility if parliamentary reform had failed, a fear confirmed by events in Europe – the year 1848 was to see the kings of France, Austria, Italy and Poland deposed.

A raft of related reforms followed. Slavery was abolished in 1833. A royal commission was set up to look at the poor laws. Robert Peel, the first leader of the Conservatives, said his party would need to 'reform to survive' and undertake the 'redress of real grievances'. Among these were the Corn Laws brought in after the Napoleonic Wars to tax imported wheat. The aim had been to protect farmers, but the effect was to price bread beyond the purse of the poor. The laws were repealed in 1846, during Peel's second administration.

Although the Swing Riots seemed to have had little effect on improving conditions for labourers at the time, their sad plight had come to the attention of people of conscience. The philanthropic Labourers' Friend Society (LFS) took up their cause with a view to providing land in some form. This fired off the powerful second Allotment Movement. At last allotments were on the political agenda.

As the situation in British farming worsened, however, desperate agricultural workers followed the example of city workers and started to set up their own friendly societies and trade unions. In 1834, six Dorset labourers attempted to form a secret trade union to protest about their wages, which had dropped from ten to six shillings a week. They were arrested and sentenced in a travesty of a trial to seven years' transportation and hard labour. Thousands marched to London in protest, to deliver a petition with 800,000 signatures pleading for the release of the Tolpuddle martyrs. The government held out for three years, then relented and granted a full pardon. The 'martyrs' returned from Australia to a hero's welcome. While labourers' demands were for better pay and shorter hours, men of influence – many of whom came from working-class backgrounds themselves – began to drive reform on allotment law as well.

**Tolpuddle martyrs**

## Labourers' Friend Society

'I am fully convinced from what I have seen of the allotment system that it is the *best* plan yet devised for improving the condition of the labourer, and for lessening pauperism'. So wrote George Curtis Rawlence of Fordingbridge to Benjamin Wills, London surgeon and founder of the Labourers' Friend Society. 'If it were more generally adopted,' continued Rawlence, 'poaching and crimes of various descriptions would decrease; and we should have the satisfaction of finding that it would make the labourers *more honest, more industrious*, and therefore cause them to become *better servants, better men* and *better Christians.*'

Benjamin Wills and like-minded liberals had wanted to do

something to help the poor at the end of the Napoleonic Wars. Their initial society held meetings at the Golden Lion pub in Smithfield and networked among other associations and the great landowners. This laid the foundation for the LFS. At its first public meeting in February 1832, the society already had between 400 and 500 members, including bishops, noblemen and MPs. Queen Victoria would become its patron, and Prince Albert its president.

**Royal patron**

*The Labourers' Friend Magazine* (originally published as *Facts and Illustrations*) aimed to influence landowners and employers. It offered advice on setting up allotments, tenancy agreements and rules. The message was to promote self-help. The labourer should 'eat the bread of independence'. Good morals would naturally follow hard work. Indeed, to avoid the faintest whiff of charity or loss of self-respect, the LFS recommended that a fair rent should be charged. Frederick Thynne, reporting to a select committee, said: 'I think it will raise the character of the labourer the moment he is put into a situation in which he can earn his own livelihood; you raise him to a respectable man when you enable him by his own industry to get "a stake in the hedge".' Those concerned also hoped to stem the tide of emigration as the provision of allotments would help raise the national output of food.

**Travelling agents**

Travelling agents were employed by the LFS to seek out the places where allotments were most needed. They were dispatched to give lectures and were highly successful in forming local societies. Mr G.W. Perry visited seven different counties (some twice) and formed seventeen local societies over two years. Mr Caldwell travelled to Ireland. Mr Henry Martin, LFS agent for West Kent, established fourteen new village societies and extended two others between 1833 and 1836.

James Orange, a pastor of Barker Gate Chapel, Nottingham, set the record. He started to promote allotments in the Midlands off his own bat and without pay, until the LFS caught up with him. In 1840 he wrote *A Plea on Behalf of the Poor*, arguing that allotments were the only way out of the poverty trap. He campaigned in the press tirelessly and lectured widely at public meetings, on one occasion to an audience of a thousand. Over two years he formed sixty-three societies in Nuneaton, Coventry, Leamington Spa and Warwick, and in the villages between Nottingham, Leicester and Derby. By 1873, Leicestershire and Nottinghamshire were third and fourth in the county allotment table, with a total of 34,809 plots.

In the year after the Swing Riots, there was a spurt of activity from Parliament on the allotment question. The first act allowed parishes to enclose up to 8 hectares/20 acres of crown land as allotments for 'spade husbandry' (hand digging). The second extended it and allowed overseers to grant allotments to 'individuals of good character'. The third act permitted enclosure awards for fuel allotments. **Action from Parliament**

A Select Committee on the Labouring Poor (Allotments of Land) in 1843, largely consisting of LFS members, concluded that allotments were 'powerful means of bettering the condition of those classes who depend for their livelihood upon their manual labour'. Plots, they recommended, should be a quarter of an acre (0.1 hectares) and close to the labourer's dwelling. Rents would be the standard rate for farmland. Taxes would fall to the landowner to pay. The report won the support of Robert Peel. The 1845 General Enclosure Act which followed (see page 84) demanded that any future enclosure of waste land should include an allowance of allotments for the poor, unless the local commissioners put up a convincing argument against it.

## The second Allotment Movement

Although this meant that the parishes were now providing allotments, the main source in the mid-nineteenth century was still the private landowner, both gentry and others, such as charities and the church. The Duke of Bedford provided 1,618 plots on his estates in Bedfordshire, Cambridgeshire, Northamptonshire and Huntingdonshire, and extended the gardens of his 1,116 cottages. The Duke of Newcastle let out 2,000 plots in Nottinghamshire, the Duke of Richmond 1,500, and the Duke of Marlborough had 900 plots on his Oxfordshire estate. In Birmingham, Lord Norton gave **The private landowner** every cottager a quarter acre of land (0.1 hectares), with the offer of another quarter if the tenant improved it.

Enthusiasm for helping the poor with land was catching. In Somerset, George Law, then Bishop of Bath and Wells, set up one of the largest allotment sites in England, of more than 40 hectares/100 acres. He rode down to visit it every day, proudly showing it to visitors. An approving letter to *The Farmer's Magazine* described it as 'a kitchen garden full of the bounties of Providence, of one hundred acres subdivided, from four to five hundred industrious, I will not call them poor, but happy allotment tenants, just now gathering in the profits of their own and children's labour.' Captain George Treweeke Scobell, later MP for Bath, founded the East Somerset LFS. Working in tandem with Bishop Law, he brought his county to the top of the league. At the first annual general meeting of the LFS, in 1832, he announced that all the Somerset clergy with the means had provided allotments.

**The bounties of Providence**

Mary Ann Gilbert, another prominent LFS member, and wife of the Board of Agriculture's chairman, was letting thirty-five allotments in Hastings, East Sussex, in 1830. After another two years the number reached 117. Her tenants always paid their rent. Deciding to expand, she attempted a daring experiment. She arranged to have topsoil spread on to a stretch of clay-covered wasteland at Beachy Head. By 1835 there were 213 allotments close to the beach. She went on to found two schools for the plot holders' children. Some twenty years later, in Hertfordshire, the forward-looking Sir John Bennet Lawes converted his estate into the Rothamsted Experimental Station, now the oldest agricultural research centre in the world. Lawes also established allotment gardens and built a social club for the plot holders.

**Cowleys**

In Derbyshire, cow pastures, or cowleys, were more popular than allotments. The women took on the dairy work.

Money was collected for the 'cow clubs' and paid out to help with bovine sickness or the loss of a cow. Some landlords provided 'cow cottages' with a dairy and cowsheds. In the 1870s, Mr Culley, an assistant parish commissioner, noted that 'it would be impossible

In Derbyshire, cow clubs were more popular than allotments.

to over-estimate the value of such a provision of milk as is within the reach of the families of most Derbyshire labourers. Many labourers in the north of Derbyshire rent with their cottages six or eight acres of grassland with a shippon [cowshed] attached, and are thus enabled to keep two cows during both summer and winter.'

Demands in the Swing Riots had been for a living wage, not land, yet there was a wild rush to take up allotments, with waiting lists running into the hundreds. It was calculated that allotments could supplement a labourer's living by 10 to 20 per cent – sometimes this could make the difference between independence and the workhouse. Arthur Ashby, in a study of rural Oxfordshire in 1913, observed that 'there is no miracle-working virtue in allotments. They cannot provide a "cure for our worst economic evils".' But, he continued, 'by the cultivation of vegetables and corn, and by feeding a pig, the labourer is enabled in a low-wage county to keep from his growing family the insistent pangs of hunger, and sometimes put a considerable barrier between himself and the poorhouse.'

The farmers caused the only stumbling block to the tide of progress. Growing wheat, they claimed, was their prerogative. Many churlishly banned it on allotments on their land and refused to sell straw for pig bedding. This was unfortunate as allotment holders generally put half the land to potatoes and the other half to wheat. Potatoes were only reluctantly being accepted as a staple food. Wheaten bread and the weekly treat of bacon were greatly prized.

**Objections from farmers**

## Potato blight

In 1845 potato blight, *Phytophthora infestans*, which quickly reduces potatoes to a disgusting mush, struck in the Isle of Wight. It was a warm, damp summer – ideal conditions for the spread of this fungal disease introduced to Europe from America. On 16 August, the *Gardeners' Chronicle* reported: 'A fatal malady has broken out among the potato crop ... In Belgium the fields are said to have been entirely desolated. There is hardly a sound sample in Covent Garden market ... As to cure for this distemper – there is none.'

Within the year it had spread throughout the mainland, where uptake of allotments slowed right down. *The Times* reported that in the Gloucestershire village of Ebrington, one in fifteen allotments had been given up. To test the market after the blight had passed through the county, a landowner, Sir Michael Hicks-Beach, put an advertisement in the local shop at Coln St Aldwyns to advertise his free plots. He did not get a single application.

Evicted family during the Great Irish Famine of the 1840s.

Then the blight hit Ireland. It was thought to be caused by 'static electricity' or 'mortiferous vapours'. In fact its severity was due to a lack of genetic variation in the types of potato the poor depended on as their main source of food. The 'lumper' potato was susceptible to blight, resulting in devastation. In the Great Irish Famine 1 million people died of disease or hunger, and some 2 million emigrated, many on the so-called 'coffin ships'. The British government under

Robert Peel (1841-1846) and Lord John Russell (1846-1852) stood by and did little to help. 'The Almighty, indeed, sent the potato blight, but the English created the famine,' as John Mitchel remarked in *The Last Conquest of Ireland* (1861).

Despite the dip in allotments caused by the blight, within a few years they were becoming an established feature of country life in Britain. Lively debate was springing up in the *Gardeners' Chronicle* between the now-literate rural workers. In one exchange, a reader calling himself the Dorset Labourer objected that he could not be expected, after a ten-hour day, to put in another four hours on an allotment. The Industrious Labourer's response was that after the land for wheat is dug and sown in autumn, and the remainder dug and cropped by March, there is little that needs doing by the labourer himself. The weeding can be done by the children, he writes, 'for nothing remunerates the cottager more than picking weeds by hand and burning them: 20 rods of potatoes do not take long to earth up, nor is it a very fatiguing job: and it is done about the end of May when the evenings are long and the weather is fine.' In his opinion, a diligent worker would think little of a sixteen-hour day, with the reward in mind of some extra bacon at the end of the week.

**To dig or not to dig**

Societies started to hold competitions with prizes – a far cry from the subsistence allotment or potato ground. In *Lark Rise to Candleford* (1939), Flora Thompson describes a nineteenth-century horticultural show in Oxfordshire where good-natured rivalry abounded:

**The horticultural show**

'Proud as they were of their celery, peas and beans, cauliflowers and marrows, and fine as were the specimens they could show of these, their potatoes were their special care, for they had to grow enough to last the year round. They grew all the old-fashioned varieties – ashleaf kidney, early rose, American rose, magnum bonum, and the huge misshaped white elephant. Everybody knew the elephant was an unsatisfactory potato, that it was awkward to handle when paring and that it boiled down to a white pulp in cooking; but it produced tubers of such astonishing size that none of the men could resist the temptation to plant it.'

By 1846 there were around 100,000 allotment plots in England alone, mostly in the poorest areas. It began to dawn on those concerned that the benefits were not merely material. William Cowper of the LFS commented on how the 'feelings of possession' could produce remarkable changes. He wrote about the working man's sense responsibility and 'the delight that arises from being able to speak of a bit of land as belonging to themselves, when they can talk of "*my* potatoes" and "*my* peas" and "*my* beans" – it gives a new current to their thoughts, and is often the commencement of that self-respect which one likes to see in their character.'

## Joseph Arch

The Labourers' Friend Society had laid the foundations for a more political campaign, which gained momentum towards the end of the century. In 1872, Joseph Arch, a hedge-cutter and Methodist preacher, launched his manifesto for better conditions for farm labourers. In an address to the villagers of Wellesbourne, in his native Warwickshire, he paid homage to the Tolpuddle martyrs – but declared that he had no intention of becoming a martyr himself. 'There is not a man here tonight,' he said, 'however poor, but likes to wear his own coat and cut his own loaf …

**Union is our hope**

Union is our hope … Ask for what is fair and when you have asked for it stand by it at all costs. Don't compromise and don't be intimidated ... Stick together and the day of your emancipation is at your own command.' If they could not get a fair day's wage for a fair day's work, they would strike.

Joseph Arch, a hedge-cutter, founded the National Agricultural Labourers' Union. Later, as Liberal MP for North West Norfolk, he worked for the labourer's 'redemption from bondage, beer, ignorance, and tyranny'.

*The Times* reported that at meetings and rallies around the country, Joseph Arch preached patience, moderation, good conduct and firmness: 'It must be in no small degree the result of his influence

A contemporary satirical print portraying the Tolpuddle martyrs begging for mercy from the king, queen and a politician who turn their backs to them while two beefeaters stand by and sneer.

that the proceedings so far have been absolutely free from disorder, large meetings of 1,500–2,000 labourers have assembled and dispersed without a blow being struck, or a stone thrown or a tipsy man being seen among the crowd.'

Within weeks, the National Agricultural Labourers' Union (NALU) was created, with Arch as president, although its funds at the time were no more than could be 'heaped in two large tea cups'. Two years later, the union had some 86,000 members, more than one-tenth of the farm labourers nationally, all paying 2d a week. NALU demands were for sixteen shillings a week and a ten-hour working day, finishing at 4p.m. on Saturdays.

The strikes started in May 1874, with 200 men in Wellesbourne. The farmers responded with a lockout, putting **Strikes & lockouts** 10,000 labourers out of work. Some strikers were sacked, others evicted from their allotments. Clergymen drowned out union meetings with their church bells. The NALU held out for five months before losing the battle, though some labourers in the South, the East and the Midlands did obtain a small increase in wages. In

Chipping Norton, Oxfordshire, sixteen women were sentenced to ten or more days' imprisonment with hard labour for harassing the strike-breakers. As they were carried off to prison in a cart, feelings had run so high that troops were called in to prevent a riot. The next day Arch spoke to a crowd of 3,000 and raised £80 to help the women.

Membership of the union dwindled to 4,254 by 1889. There were suspicions about the maladministration of union funds. Disillusioned and defeated, Arch changed tack and joined the Liberal Party, where his declared aim was to bring 'redemption from bondage, beer, ignorance, and tyranny'. Concerned to extend voting rights to the rural labourer, he helped work on the **Third Reform Act**, which was made law in 1884. Seven million men by virtue of being a householder of a year's continuous residency at the same address, and a further million on other grounds, were now enfranchised – 60 per cent of the adult male population.

This reform changed the outlook for allotments, as Whigs and Conservatives would now be competing against each other to win the country vote. When Arch was elected MP for North-West Norfolk in 1885 he used his maiden speech to put forward his views on land for labourers. To allow him to rise above pauper level, a labourer needed 'some scope for his ability'. He 'should have a good quarter of an acre attached to his cottage; and if he can cultivate it and get enough out of it to take another half acre, it would be a wise step for any landed proprietor to let thrifty and persevering men have it.'

## Jesse Collings

The situation in the country was reaching crisis point. The repeal of the Corn Laws in 1846 had resulted in cheap corn flooding in from America, undercutting the British grower. By the end of the nineteenth century wheat acreage had dropped by half. Farm workers were abandoning rural life in droves. Thousands were emigrating to the colonies.

Jesse Collings, son of a Birmingham bricklayer and friend of Joseph Arch, resolved to see what he could do to improve the lot of the farm labourer. His concern for the state of the countryside stemmed from his travels as an ironmongery salesman. In 1882, as Liberal MP for Ipswich, Collings succeeded in getting the Allotments Extension Act through. The aim was to prevent the Poor Law Commissioners and charity trustees dodging their obligation to lease land allocated for allotments. The act gave workers the right to complain to the Charity Commissioners, who in turn now had the authority to ensure compliance. But there was a flaw – the commissioners charged with this role were not impartial. They were interested parties. Jesse Collings realized that without an association to drive things forward, the act would be totally ineffectual.

**Allotments Extension Act**

To ensure that attention remained focused, Collings then formed the Allotments Extension Association (later the Allotments and Smallholdings Association). Its purpose, he said, was to 'help working men who cannot succeed in getting trustees of charity lands to let allotments'. In 1888 he was instrumental in founding the Rural Labourers' League, which eventually employed twenty-five local agents and had 3,000 volunteers across the country. Ultimately, the result of the act was a new national total of nearly 400,000 smallholdings of under 1.6 hectares/4 acres, and more than 270,000 'garden' allotments.

Collings belonged to a powerful group of land reformers that included Joseph Chamberlain – 'radical Joe', once mayor of Birmingham and president of the Board of Trade – and John Bright, a Quaker and politician. Together they campaigned for 'three acres and a cow' to fulfil the basic needs of a labourer and his family. This became the slogan of their movement, causing some amusement among the Conservatives.

**Three acres & a cow**

In 1886, Collings brought down Lord Salisbury's government over the allotment question. He suggested an amendment to the Queen's Speech, regretting that the Conservatives had no plans to help agricultural labourers find allotments and smallholdings. William Gladstone stood up to support this move, and promised to 'restore the old local communities of the country'. The dramatic outcome was recounted by Lord Fortescue in *Poor Men's Gardens* (1888): 'An amendment to the address about allotments, moved by

Mr Jesse Collings in January 1886, and carried by the votes
of the bulk of the Liberal members, obliged Lord Salisbury
to resign and restored Mr Gladstone to power. Once in office,
however, Mr Gladstone did nothing whatever to promote the
extension of allotments.'

Collings' *coup de grâce* was the 1887 Allotments Act. Local
authorities were now obliged to provide allotments if any six registered
local voters requested them and where there was no provision. This
key phrase is the basis of modern allotment law and has saved many
a site from developers. It means that allotments are today virtually
a citizen's right. However, at the time, as Frederick Ernest Green
pointed out in *A History of the English Agricultural Labourer, 1870–
1920* (1920), 'whilst this was of some benefit to urban workers who
could display more independence of spirit, it required some courage
for agricultural labourers to send in a request to a Board of Guardians
composed chiefly of farmers hostile to the granting of allotments.'

Both Collings and Chamberlain left the Liberal Party over the
question of Irish home rule, which they opposed, but in 1919 Collings
was to see his lifelong project come to fruition with an amendment to
the Land Settlement Bill for demobilized servicemen. This allowed
smallholders to buy land on credit, another concern he had toiled on
over the years.

In his book *Landlords and Allotments* (1886), Lord Onslow,
president of the Board of Agriculture from 1903, describes how
much perceptions of allotments had now changed. They were no
longer there to provide extra rations for a hand-to-mouth existence,
or for giving the hapless labourer 'a stake in the hedge'. They

should simply be for leisure, because what mattered to the
labourer was a regular wage. As for cow pastures, it was unwise
to assume that the wife would be capable or even willing to do
the dairy work. In contrast to those of his forebears who took the high
moral ground, Onslow recommended that no one should be turned
away for their idleness or 'dissolute habits'. Having the care of an
allotment and complying with the rules, he believed, could well be the
making of just such a man.

Returning home.

The year 1908 brought in the key Small Holdings and Allotments Act, the basis of today's allotment law. It endorsed Collings' 1887 act, obliging local authorities to provide sufficient allotments and giving them powers to make compulsory purchases of land where necessary. They also had the right to sell allotment sites if 'no longer needed' – a clause open to interpretation. In 1913 the Land Enquiry Committee estimated that two-thirds of parishes had allotments, with the great majority in the south, and that virtually any labourer could obtain one.

So, allotments were finally accepted. The trade unions, including the Trades Union Congress, founded in 1868, and the National Farmers' Union, founded in 1908, with their labouring membership, were making themselves heard. In addition, no longer was it the landed gentry who were calling the shots and providing the land. It was the local authorities. By mid-century, the Labourers' Friend Society also felt that it had made its mark. Its members had done great service to forwarding the allotment cause. The LFS reinvented itself in 1844 as the Society for Improving the Condition of the Labouring Classes (eventually absorbed into the Peabody Trust in the 1960s), and turned its attention to the next cause of greatest need – housing in the inner cities.

# 8. INDUSTRY, POPULAR PROTEST & HOW ALLOTMENTS LEFT THE COUNTRY FOR THE CITY 1800–1914

Our lives are not your sheaves to glean—
Our rights your bales to barter:
Give all their own—from cot to throne,
But ours shall be THE CHARTER!
*Ernest Jones, 'A Chartist Chorus' (1846)*

The Victorian era was a period of prosperity and peace – the Pax Britannica. Although Britain was involved in the Crimean and Boer Wars, Europe remained peaceful for the hundred years between the end of the Napoleonic Wars in 1815 and the outbreak of the First World War in 1914. With the largest empire that had ever existed, Britain was now the leading industrial nation, producing more than half of the world's iron, coal and cotton.

There was a cost, however. Free trade, although vastly profitable, was causing a near death blow to British farming. By the 1880s, 80 per cent of wheat was coming in from America and Russia. Unemployed labourers were abandoning the countryside at the rate of 30,000 a year. The census of 1801 showed that 50 per cent of the population was living in towns. While in 1750 this figure had been just 15 per cent, by 1880 it would rise to 80 per cent. London's population alone doubled in size between 1800 and 1850, from 1 to 2 million. The main growth, though, was in the huge industrial cities in the Midlands and

Urban poor getting their water from a pump in the street.

the North – Leeds, Liverpool, Manchester, Bradford, Birmingham, Newcastle and Glasgow.

Victorian Britain was a two-tier society. The urban poor lived in the dire squalor and poverty so vividly described by Dickens. They included thousands of immigrants from Ireland, along with unwanted children, working in inhumane conditions in factories and housed in ghettos. The huge advances in technology – famously celebrated in the Great Exhibition of 1851 – had caused wide unemployment in the industrial towns. Country people pouring into the cities to seek work found little respite from their troubles.

As a result, the nineteenth century was pitted with frequent and violent revolts. At times, the price of bread went beyond the reach of the poor, provoking a spate of 'Bread or Blood' riots. These were often led by Luddite textile artisans, but were joined by country labourers,

MICROCOSM dedicated to the London Water Companies

MONSTER SOUP commonly called THAMES WATER, being a correct representation of that precious stuff doled out to us!!

Cartoon by William Heath of the polluted River Thames that caused the 'Great Stink' of 1858.

colliery workers – even women – all desperately looking to feed their families. Working people were also becoming increasingly vociferous in their demands for a fairer society. Had the Great Reform Act not finally been passed in 1832, there were plans for a protest march 200,000 strong.

**Cramped housing & cholera**

Overcrowding and insanitary conditions in industrial cities caused three massive waves of infectious disease in the 1830s and 1840s. Cholera, typhoid fever, typhus, tuberculosis, smallpox, scarlet fever and influenza epidemics were accompanied by dysentery, caused by flies feeding on the manure that littered the streets and human waste that oozed out of inadequate sewers. Between 1836 and 1842, the death toll from cholera alone was 52,000 in Britain. In his *Report on the Sanitary Condition of the Labouring Population of Great Britain* (1842), Edwin Chadwick, secretary to the Poor Law Commission, calculated that for every person who died of

This 1832 etching mocks the fruitless attempts to take preventative measures against cholera.

old age or violence in 1839, eight died of 'specific' diseases. Medicine seemed to have advanced little since the Black Death in the fourteenth century. It was still believed that cholera was caused by 'miasmas', or infected air. Not until the late nineteenth century did it begin to dawn on the medical profession that polluted water was the culprit.

**The Great Stink**

Little was done about London's public health hazards for reasons of expense until the Great Stink of 1858. This occurred in a scorching summer when the abominable stench of untreated sewage cooking in the Thames so overwhelmed Parliament that they resorted to soaking the curtains in bleach and considered relocating to Hampton Court. Instead, they legislated at speed. The Treasury dug into the coffers to invest in the massive sewage system that is still in operation today. Quite possibly, this experience may have triggered some of the more enlightened councils, such as Sheffield and Birmingham, to provide allotments or small gardens for residents to get out of the smelly cities and enjoy the fresh air – though these were mostly for the middle classes at the time.

## Trouble in Britain's industrial heartland

As anger mounted in the face of disease, unemployment, hunger and hopelessness in the cities, inevitably there was protest from the poor. Wool, linen and cloth manufacture were the lifeblood of West Yorkshire, Cheshire, Lancashire and the Midlands, particularly Nottingham, Leicester and Derby, and had been so since the days of Edward III's woolsack. In the early nineteenth century, however, the skilled textile workers were being replaced by machines such as the stocking frame and power loom. All could be operated by unskilled workers on low pay.

**Mechanization & King Ludd**

The Luddites, fearsome revolutionaries, vented their fury in the face of these changes. Their leader was the mythical figure of 'General' or 'King' Ludd, supposedly named after a champion stocking-frame smasher. Between 1811 and 1816 they left death threats written in blood, set buildings on fire and vandalized machines. In 1812, when wheat prices soared, there were Bread or Blood riots in Manchester, Oldham, Ashton, Rochdale, Stockport and Macclesfield.

An 1812 engraving of Captain Ludd, mythical leader of the Luddites, disguised as a woman and rallying his rebels.

Bread was still the staff of life, but the price of wheat fluctuated according to the weather, the harvests, wars with France and the price regulations imposed by the government. Farmers who hoarded wheat in the hope of a price rise were forced to go to market by gangs of Luddites. The countryside was scoured in search of stashed stores. Mills and houses were raided. There were funereal parades with bread stuck on poles, draped in black crape. It was said that it took more soldiers to quell them than were fighting Napoleon on the Iberian peninsula.

**Death of William Horsfall**

Crisis point was reached in the West Riding, following a wave of 'cropper' redundancies. The croppers were men of skill and strength who wielded massive shears to 'finish' the cloth as part of an extensive and long-standing cottage industry. During an ambush near Huddersfield in April 1812, William Horsfall, a mill owner who swore he would 'ride up to the saddle girths in Luddite blood', was shot dead. In the aftermath, the government charged sixty men, not all of them Luddites. Vicious sentences were meted out to set an example. Three men were hanged at York for Horsfall's murder. Fourteen others, who had attacked and besieged a West Riding mill, were hanged a week later. Lord Sidmouth, the home secretary, and Lord Ellenborough, chief justice, anticipated the 'happiest effects in various parts of the kingdom' as a result of the executions.

An emergency bill was brought in to make machine-breaking a capital offence for a limited period from March 1812. Lord Byron, who opposed the bill, devoted his maiden speech in February of that year to the Luddites' defence: 'Whilst these outrages must be admitted to exist to an alarming extent, it cannot be denied that they have arisen from circumstances of the most unparalleled distress ... nothing but absolute want could have driven a large, and once honest and industrious, body of the people into the commission of excesses so hazardous to themselves, their families, and the community.' In 1816 violence resurged when fifty-three frames were smashed at mills in Loughborough following a bad harvest and a drop in trade. Troops were called in. Six rioters were executed and another three were transported. Luddism finally subsided after this, but the Swing Riots – the country version of the Luddite revolts – would soon follow suit.

**Lord Byron's speech**

## The union workhouse

Less than twenty years later, anger again flared up, provoked by the new Poor Law introduced in 1834 to cut the ever-rising burden of poor relief. It wiped out all former poor laws apart from the 1662 Settlement and Removal Act, which tied people seeking poor relief to their parishes of origin (see page 59). The only help henceforth for the able-bodied would be the workhouse. Smaller parishes would join together to establish 'union' workhouses.

The outcry came first from the countryside, following a bitter winter that forced many to apply for relief. Disturbances broke out in East Anglia and in the South, only dispersed when the Riot Act was read out. This had been introduced in 1715 to prevent 'tumults and riotous assemblies', giving the army *carte blanche* to deal with groups of twelve or more that did not disperse within the hour. Protest was more effective in the North, with the press campaigns and pamphleteering organized by Michael Sadler, Tory MP for Aldborough, Yorkshire, and his friend Richard Oastler, known as the 'Factory King'. As well as being opposed to the new

**Anti-poor law movement**

The workhouse. George Cruikshank's famous illustration of Oliver Twist asking for more, from the original first installment of the novel published in *Bentley's Miscellany* between 1837 and 1839.

poor law, both were driving reform for the ten-hour day and fighting to improve the cruel conditions for children in factories. Sadler was also vociferous in promoting allotments for the labouring poor. In 1831 he proposed that parish authorities build cottages with gardens, provide allotments large enough to keep a cow, and make parish land available for the unemployed.

Other critics of the workhouse system included William Cobbett, now MP for Oldham. His 1835 pamphlet, *Legacy to Labourers*, viewed the poor law as an attack on the traditional social compact between the propertied and the poor. He deplored the humiliating badges that paupers were forced to wear in the workhouses, and the splitting up of families – which, as rumour had it, was a wicked Malthusian plot to prevent the poor from 'breeding'. The economist Thomas Attwood, a leading light in political reform, described the workhouses as prisons for the poor – a sentiment shared by the inmates, who referred to them as the Bastille or 'Old Basty'. In 1845 *The Times* exposed the scandal of the Andover workhouse, where starving inmates had resorted to eating the bones they were crushing for fertilizer. It led to the replacement of the Poor Law Commission by a more accountable Poor Law Board.

The nineteenth century also saw the emergence of the Chartist movement, the first mass working-class political party.

**Peterloo massacre & Chartism**

The Peterloo Massacre, where troops charged into a crowd of 60,000 peaceful protesters at St Peter's Field in Manchester. Cartoon by George Cruikshank.

It was formed in 1838, in the wake of the Great Reform Act of 1832 that enfranchised the middle classes to one in six males (compared to one per hundred in France). The militant working classes saw this as a feeble compromise. Frustration at being powerless to vote was intense. The 'People's Charter' demanded that all males over twenty-one be enfranchised. It also called for secret ballots, salaries for MPs, constituencies of equal numbers and annual elections.

The rise of Chartism had been given impetus by a tragic event back in 1819, when the radical Manchester Patriotic Union held a rally attended by more than 60,000 people at St Peter's Field. Through a series of misunderstandings, the cavalry (reportedly drunk) had charged at the crowds with their sabres, killing eleven and injuring hundreds of innocents in what came to be called the Peterloo Massacre.

Feargus O'Connor, an Irish Protestant of the landowning class, MP for County Cork and a prominent member of the Chartist movement, had a radical agenda. In 1836 he joined the London Working Men's Association and a year later started the *Northern Star*, a weekly newspaper which quickly gained a circulation of 48,000. His fiery speeches promising to lead people to 'death or glory' caused him to fall out with more moderate Chartist leaders, who considered him a rabble-rouser. He was later tried for seditious libel at York and imprisoned for eighteen months, but continued to edit the *Northern Star* from his prison cell.

**Feargus O'Connor**

Three Chartist petitions were presented to Parliament between 1839 and 1848. The last famously followed a public meeting, allegedly of 50,000, on Kennington Common, London. The Chartists claimed to have some 6 million signatures. When it turned out that there were fewer than 2 million, and many were forged (including Queen Victoria's), the movement lost credibility. Nonetheless, the Second Reform Act in 1867 doubled the suffrage to two out of five adult males, with a property qualification.

**Bogus signatures**

## Land experiments & city allotments

An interesting project set up by O'Connor in 1845 was the Chartist Cooperative Land Society (later the National Land Society). The aim was to establish urban workers (rather than country labourers) as smallholders with a cottage and 0.8 to 1.6 hectares/2 to 4 acres. The society had some 70,000 members who paid small amounts towards an eventual £2.10s share and the chance of getting a plot on a ballot system. Although set up in good faith, the scheme was shut down in 1851 as an illegal lottery.

**Chartist Cooperative Land Society**

Five Chartist communities were also founded. One did well. At Great Dodford, in Worcestershire, after a rocky start, the smallholders started a profitable market garden business. While keeping their own trades going just in case, they grew and sold garlic to the sauce manufacturers Lea & Perrins, in Worcester, and marketed flowers, peas, beans and shallots. Each year they held a 'strawberry wake' where, for 6d, you could pick as much as you could eat – a tradition that continued until 1922.

Allotments were slow to come to the city poor, although gardens to rent were provided for artisans and tradesmen from the early eighteenth century. Sheffield, the prosperous steel town, had established more than 1,000 allotments in the outskirts as early as the 1780s – the first town to provide them in such large numbers. They were taken up by cutlers, button makers, innkeepers, tailors, bricklayers and the like.

**Guinea gardens**

Birmingham pioneered the even more upmarket 'guinea gardens' (multiples of guineas being the ground rent) from the 1730s, and within the century there were 2,000 on the city's outskirts. These leisure gardens were treasured and handed down through the generations by residents mostly engaged in manufacture and trade. William Hutton, in his *History of Birmingham* (1783), writes approvingly: 'Health and amusement are found in the prodigious number of private gardens scattered round Birmingham, from which we often behold the father returning with a cabbage, and the daughter with a nosegay.'

Some guinea gardens had summerhouses, pavilions and arbours. There were orchards and flower borders. Birmingham was all too briefly a city of beautiful gardens. John Claudius Loudon, the celebrated Victorian garden author, expressed astonishment in the *Gardener's Magazine* at the range of plants he had seen on a visit to a guinea garden in 1831. Similar schemes were taken up in Nottingham, Warwick, Coventry and Newcastle.

In the mid-nineteenth century, 2 hectares/5 acres of land at Birmingham's botanic garden were given over to allotments. More were to be found in Newcastle, on the space beneath the Central Motorway now occupied by the university campus. In those days, the site was on the banks of Pandon Burn, a picturesque ravine. The plots here were attached to pit cottages in the outlying mining villages.

**Rowntree allotments**

The emergence of allotments owes much to acts of charity by enlightened individuals. By the turn of the century, paternalistic private businesses began to provide plots for their workers. An outstanding example was Rowntree, the family-owned

A 1905 publication aimed at amateur gardeners and allotment holders.

The Edwardian allotment. The top picture shows how an allotment might look prior to the rule that they were to be mainly for vegetables.

Quaker chocolate factory in York. In 1901 they had taken a survey which showed that one-fifth of the city's population had less food than the inmates of York's union workhouse. In consequence, the family decided to give their 4,000 employees a model village, schools and allotments.

When the great engineer George Stephenson, known as 'father of the railways', founded his company (later the Clay Cross Company) near Chesterfield in the 1830s, employing miners to dig for coal, iron ore and limestone, he built them a school and houses with gardens. He also provided allotments and pleasure gardens 'to foster a love of home' among his workers. The company provided lime from the mines to improve the soil for their vegetables.

The government of the day was beginning to realize that allotments could bring great benefits to the poor at relatively little cost. The first official census of allotments was carried out in 1873. It concluded that there were 344,712 plots across the country (similar to the current estimated total of 300,000 in the twenty-first century). However, since calculations were based on the agricultural returns and did not include urban plots, this figure had to be a very low estimate. The census of the Board of Agriculture in 1890 recorded 441,024 plots in England, 6,410 in Scotland and 7,562 in Wales. Writing in the *Royal Commission on Labour* (1894), W.C. Little noted that allotments were reportedly unpopular in Wales, but that 'potato grounds were to be found everywhere and gardens are very commonly attached to cottages.'

**First official census**

Toward the end of the nineteenth century, living conditions were slowly beginning to improve. David Lloyd George, chancellor to the Asquith administration between 1908 and 1915, was determined to 'lift the shadow of the workhouse from the homes of the poor'. His hope was 'that before this generation has passed away, we shall have advanced a great step towards that good time, when poverty, and the wretchedness and human degradation which always follows in its camp, will be as remote to the people of this country as the wolves which once infested its forests.'

Lloyd George introduced a raft of reforms anticipating the

Punch cartoon entitled 'Snowed Under', depicting David Lloyd George with his St Bernard puppy in 1920. The dog (to his master): 'This situation appeals to my hereditary instincts. Shall I come to the rescue?'

welfare state. The Old Age Pensions Act of 1908 helped clear the workhouses. The National Insurance Act was the first step toward a means-tested pension for people over seventy. The scheme also provided sickness and maternity benefit, and free medical treatment. Some 13 million workers were compulsorily covered. Workers earning less than £160 per year had to pay 4d a week towards the scheme. The employer contributed 3d and the government 2d. When Lloyd George was heckled by workers chanting 'Taffy was a Welshman, Taffy was a thief', his riposte was 'Ninepence for four pence!' The Labour Exchange was introduced in 1909 to pay out benefits and advertise jobs. It became illegal to sell children tobacco, alcohol and fireworks, to allow them to work in dangerous trades or send them out to beg. Reforms were brought in for the factories and mines.

Without the dire necessity to do so, country labourers were no longer quite so keen to put in extra hours on the plot. By the time war was declared in 1914, it was reckoned that one-quarter of allotments were now in the towns and cities. Soon there would be a complete turnaround. Allotments would become few and far apart in the countryside, but would be a regular feature of the urban landscape, particularly in city suburbs and mining towns.

# 9. DIGGING FOR DORA – ALLOTMENTS & THE WAR EFFORT 1914–1918

London's wartime allotments 'raised cabbages
from concrete and broad beans from brickbats'.

*Rowland Prothero (1918)*

Pax Britannica came to an abrupt end when a Serbian nationalist assassinated the heir to the Austro–Hungarian throne, Archduke Franz Ferdinand, in Sarajevo on 28 June 1914. In retaliation, Austria shelled Belgrade. As Russia mobilized to retaliate, Kaiser Wilhelm II, emperor of Germany, declared war against Russia and invaded Luxembourg and Belgium before moving on to France. As Britain was part of the 1907 Triple Entente with Russia and France (counterbalanced by the alliance between Austria, Germany and Italy), and had also been party to the creation of Belgium in 1831, the country, under Herbert Henry Asquith, had little choice but to declare war on Germany.

Of great concern to Britain was the possibility that Germany would cut off imports by taking control of the North Sea and blocking the Channel ports. Robert Peel's profitable free trade policy had provided cheap bread since the 1840s, but meant that the country now relied on imports for a third of its food, including 70 per cent of cereals and cheese, 80 per cent of fruit and 100 per cent of sugar.

During the first years of the war, imports continued to reach Britain and there was no immediate crisis over food. By the spring of 1917, however, the picture was very different.

**U-boat
campaign**

One defence against the U-boat campaign was multicoloured 'dazzle camouflage' to make ships more difficult to identify and target. Here, the SS *Olympic* – nicknamed 'Old Reliable' for having transported 200,000 troops during the war – finally comes into harbour.

Germany had declared unrestricted submarine warfare. In February and March, their U-boats had sunk around 500,000 tons of merchant shipping in the Atlantic, and an unprecedented 860,000 tons in April. As a result, Britain was within six weeks of running out of wheat and four days of running out of sugar. Lord Devonport, appointed the first food controller at the new Ministry of Food, stated: 'The enemy is trying to take away our daily bread. He is sinking our wheat ships. If he succeeds in starving us, our soldiers will have died in vain.'

The previous summer there had been a wheat-crop failure

in the UK and North America, adding to the now desperate pressure on food supplies. Agriculture had hit rock bottom. All farm hands had signed up, creating a shortage of labour on the land. The army had even taken the horses. Now, instead of allotments being seen as a privilege, suddenly they were a vital way to help feed the nation and win the war. The public were prevailed upon to get growing. This they did, to such an extent that the *Spectator* could comment on 5 September 1919: 'From a position of lowliness in public estimation allotment-holders have risen suddenly to one of National Importance.'

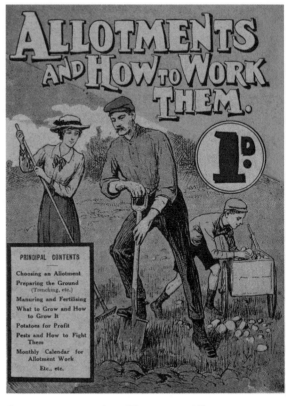

A one-penny magazine, *Allotments and How to Work Them*.

## Allotment fever

Asquith, who had unwisely declared in July 1915 that there was not 'the least fear that any probable or conceivable development of German submarine activity can be a serious menace to our food supply', was replaced as prime minister by David Lloyd George in a parliamentary coup. In April 1917 Lloyd George began to turn the tide of merchant navy losses by insisting – against the strongest advice of the Admiralty, who were loath to spare their destroyers and warships – that merchant ships

**Asquith resigns**

must be protected by a convoy of the Royal Navy.

Meanwhile, the government was taking steps to increase the quantity of home-produced food. In November 1916, the Vacant Land Cultivation Society (VLCS), was unexpectedly summoned to a meeting by the president of the Board of Agriculture, Lord Crawford. The VLCS was a charity founded by American soap millionaire and philanthropist, Joseph Fels, who had moved to England in 1901. He aimed to get waste land put into cultivation by the unemployed – a marriage of 'idle land with idle labour'. Since its foundation in 1907, the VLCS had made few inroads due to the 'lack of sympathy' of landowners and the 'customary wet blanket' of officialdom. That was about to change.

**Vacant Land Cultivation Society**

When Gerald Butcher, the charity's superintendent and instructor, left the meeting a little more than an hour later, he realized that 'probably the greatest drama which had taken place in land reform for many generations was about to be enacted.' He was referring to the government's imminent plan to extend the already broad war powers provided under the 1914 Defence of the Realm Act (DORA). The new Cultivation of Lands Order would allow the government to seize all unrated or unoccupied land for farming and allotments without the consent – or even the knowledge – of the owner.

The VLCS, as a charitable organization, was pulled in to work in tandem with the councils and parks' committees on the establishment of allotments.

Within six months of the order becoming law, membership of the VLCS rose from 80 to 8,000. Allotment fever – 'allotmentitis' according to the press – seized the country. There was a great rush by the civilian population to help the war effort by 'Digging for DORA'. 'Morning noon and night,' wrote Butcher, 'allotment authorities and local societies were bombarded by those anxious to partake in the great adventure.' He received requests for advice from 'all parts of the kingdom'.

Demand in Birmingham ran into so many thousands that the city was divided into different areas, each with a supervisor to organize plots and help new growers. This worked so well

**Birmingham's example**

and the produce looked so good that it was said to encourage others to have a go.

In London, however, there was some unpatriotic resistance. In Kensington and around elegant areas of west London, residents flatly refused to allow their leafy locked squares to be marred by vegetable-growing. More surprisingly, the London County Council (LCC) failed to cooperate, as the VLCS was to discover at the start of its first wartime project, at the Furzedown Estate in Tooting. Hundreds of applicants had been waiting for weeks to get digging and an order for the land had been put in place. The LCC did nothing but make lame excuses, which in January 1917 the *London Evening News* decided to expose to readers:

# Allotments.

IT COST ME MONEY, WEEKS OF TOIL,
IN RAIN, AND WIND, AND SUN,
AND NOW I'VE DUG THE TATIES UP,
I'VE ONLY GROWN JUST ONE.

Man with a single potato. One of the many humorous cartoons of the First World War.

'There was a shortage of food in the land, and the State called upon all its citizens earnestly to cultivate such soil as lay ready to their hands. To this end the Local Bodies were urged to make a record of all vacant land under their respective jurisdictions and to parcel it out among those who were willing to help in making it bear the crops which were so sorely needed.

'Many bodies at this work fell upon the task, so that in quite a short space of time there were men digging with spades and enthusiasm to prepare soil for the harvest. But the LCC, being a Great Body, merely

Petty officers on allotments at anchorage. The *Illustrated War News* of July 1917 reported that 'For all ratings in the Grand Fleet, in the immediate neighbourhood of harbours it uses, ground is provided as allotments.'

referred the matter to a Committee, which discussed it with another Committee, which disagreed with everything the first Committee had said, so that in the end the only crop which was raised was a crop of objections.'

Wandsworth, Lambeth and Woolwich took the lead by applying directly to the Board of Agriculture, overruling the LCC, and succeeded in getting 156 hectares/386 acres released for allotments. Other local London councils followed suit. Unpromising sites were cleared of tons of rubbish and turned into successful vegetable gardens. A typical challenge was a site in Battersea formerly used as a 'shoot' for dust carts. Battersea council regarded the idea of growing vegetables on it as 'sheer madness', and quoted the local MP as saying that you could not even grow a 'consumptive cabbage' in London. Over 80 tons of refuse were wheeled off the site by hand, and it was slowly transformed into beautifully tidy and fruitful plots.

Gerald Butcher's *Allotments for All: The Story of a Great Movement* (1918) recalls the experience of a Londoner allotted a plot on the very spot once occupied by a fairground roundabout: 'When I began to dig, I found the soil rich with iron bolts, sheet iron, brickbats, broken bottles, china, old boots, oyster shells and rags. But I hacked my way through, and now, with winter coming on, I thank God for the abundance He has given me.' Near Pentonville prison, a 'miracle' was achieved by four 'hard working men' on thin unproductive soil covering a railway tunnel. The site, surrounded by a brick wall, was baking hot in summer – conditions not improved by the revolting stink coming from the tripe factory next door.

Peter Anderson Graham, editor of *Country Life* in 1917, noticed on his travels a piece of waste ground used as a dump, where a 'feeble old man, looking quite past work' was digging. He was joined by others 'equally grey and feeble, some even halt and blind'. Graham remarked that they clearly 'knew something of tillage' and worked hard, with 'a touch of that neatness which characterizes the English cottage gardener'. Sometimes they got help from small children. 'Old and young sallied out' to scrape manure off the roads and cart it back in an old wheelbarrow or pram – with the result that the plants were "growing splendidly". 'Who', Graham asked, 'could have expected the earth to yield up her treasures of food to patriarchs and babies?'

"Hi! Billy, come on, let's foller 'im."

"Wot for?"

"Spuds! Why, 'e might skid."

Original wartime ink drawing cartoon signed by F. R. Bolton and sent to his niece Elsie Bolton in 1917.

Gerald Butcher denied that he was trying to turn the country into 'a giant cabbage patch'. Even if every man were given a plot of ten rods (253 square metres), this would still only have covered one ninety-sixth of the surface of Britain. Yet there was never enough land to satisfy the waiting lists – for each lucky applicant, there were six left on hold. In London, hundreds of people, from all branches of society, were being allocated plots every week. They were instructed to arrive with a spade and string, usually on a Saturday afternoon. Many plot-holders had never grown anything before and would not have known 'a bed of turnips from a bed of beets', according to Butcher.

**Novice growers**

It was usually female war-workers who helped get people started. A visitor to a site in Putney was struck by the scene of women measuring and marking out the plots, and wrote this verse in celebration:

Oh England! No more barren ground
Shall e'er disgrace thy countryside –
Diana bids such wastes provide
Potatoes plump, and carrots slender,
Parsnips, succulent and tender.
Stout cauliflowers, and portly cabbage,
Gay Brussels sprouts and sombre spinach;
Thus would she help thee keep each day
The German hunger-wolf at bay.

**Royal war effort**

George V had vegetable plots put in at Buckingham Palace and Windsor Castle, and dispatched his lunchtime guests to work on them. Model allotments were set up beside the Albert Memorial (where the king insisted that vegetables take the place of red geraniums) and near the zoo, with park gardeners on hand to give advice. These were so successful that the LCC stopped dragging its feet and put in model allotments in six other parks. Tomatoes were grown in their greenhouses, and the bedding-out was replaced with vegetables to be sold cheaply to the public. School playing fields were also dug up.

The government told people to lobby their local councils for more ground, and urged local authorities to find money for morale-boosting prizes for the best kept plot or the finest vegetables. Lloyd George, who claimed to be an enthusiastic potato-grower at his home near Walton Heath, in Surrey, encouraged the country to get digging. In March 1917 he underlined how critical the situation was: 'If you can use a spade – go on to the land at once. Go to help replenish our dangerously low stocks. Go now while there is still time for the spring sowings to yield you summer and winter food ... It is essential for the safety of the nation, for the life of the nation, that we should put forth immediately every effort to increase production.' The Archbishop of Canterbury let it be known that the Church of England permitted work on allotments on Sundays.

**The railways**

It was at this time that the railway companies, with land to spare, became a major provider of allotments. They had in peacetime already allowed staff in quiet countryside stations to cultivate a plot between train arrivals. They now increased the number of railway plots to 6,000, bought gardening essentials in bulk and sold them on at cost. They held shows and competitions. The standard was reported to be gratifyingly high, and the range of varieties, impressive. Proceeds, sometimes raised by auction at the end of the show, would go to the railway orphans' fund or to buy cigarettes for the war wounded. Excess produce was often sent to hospitals.

The Agricultural Organization Society (AOS), a charity founded in 1901 to improve cooperative food production, also upped its game. The role of the AOS was to liaise closely with the relevant government departments and give free legal advice to farmers, smallholders and allotment societies on setting up cooperatives. It had a board of eminent governors – Francis Acland and Lord Bledisloe, both former parliamentary secretaries to the Board of Agriculture, and Lady Denman from the Women's Land Army. In response to the war effort, the AOS created a new Allotments and Smallholdings Department to help plot holders with the business side of setting up allotments. They produced literature with tips on management and sample regulations. By the end of the war, 400 allotment societies were affiliated under the AOS umbrella, with a total membership of 60,000.

## More hands to the plough

While allotments were doing a grand job on a degree of public self-sufficiency, the government's absolute priority was to increase farming output. With this in mind, County War Agricultural Executive Committees (War Ags) were established in England and Wales in the autumn of 1915. They were drawn from the farming communities, landowners and local people. Their job was to liaise between government and farmers in order to manage the country's agricultural resources effectively. More hands were urgently needed on the land, especially since the government took over extra land for farming – 1.2 million hectares/3 million acres by 1918. At the start of the war, 72,000 soldiers had been put to work on farms. The Food Production Department later recruited 30,000

*The War Ags*

Although the Women's Land Army was not started until 1917, when 40,000 men lent by the army to work the farms left for the battlefields, women had already stepped into their shoes.

prisoners of war. The workforce also counted 4,000 volunteers and 'other labour' (which included conscientious objectors), 300,000 part-time women workers and 15,000 schoolboys.

The War Ags, the government and various women's organizations had been attempting to encourage women to work on the land since the beginning of the war.

**The lilac sunbonnet brigade**

In 1916, the Women's National Land Service Corps was formed. The chair, Louisa Wilkins OBE, decided not to approach women who had to earn their living, as the pay offered by the corps was too low. She would instead be enlisting 'those with secondary education', who would join the scheme with 'patriotic motives'. These select few would quite often be sent off by farmers to get the local village women to join 'by persuasion or example'. The eventual 2,000 volunteers were given light farm work, such as milking or butter-making. They were mercilessly lampooned and laughed at by the press, who dubbed them the 'lilac sunbonnet brigade' – something of a mystery, as they had no uniform other than armbands. The official advice, however, was to purchase a special 'farm outfit' from Harrods.

By the time food shortages hit in 1917, more substantial help was needed. The Women's Land Army (WLA), started up in January that year, was led by Muriel Talbot, director of the Women's Branch of the Food Production Department, with Lady Gertrude Denman as her honorary assistant. A 1917 issue of the *Monthly Labor Review* explained this initiative to its American readership: 'In Great Britain the services of women on land will be more imperatively needed than ever owing to the withdrawal at the end of May of the 40,000 soldiers lent by the army to do the spring work in the fields.' The report went on to outline how the new WLA 'is being greatly helped by the existence of a small nucleus of trained women, or at least of women with some experience on the land, known as the Women's National Land Service Corps.'

**The Women's Land Army**

Lady Denman was a powerhouse, and would take over as head of the WLA during the Second World War. She was active in the Family Planning Association and the National Federation of Women's Institutes. In 1916 she had chaired the Smokes for Soldiers and Sailors Society, using her own ballroom as a packaging centre. By the time she left the society, 265 million cigarettes had been given out to injured servicemen on hospital trains and ships.

It was something of a novelty for women to work on the land. The WLA handbooks advised: 'You are doing a man's work and so you are dressed rather like a man; but remember that just because you wear a smock and breeches you should take care to behave like a British girl who expects chivalry and respect from everyone she meets.' Within a year, the WLA had signed up 23,000 land girls to take over what had traditionally been men's work. Muriel Talbot reported in *The Times* that among her recruits were 5,734 milkers, 293 tractor drivers, 3,971 field workers, 635 carters, 260 plough women, 84 thatchers and 21 shepherds. That did not include the 1,000 girls trained to catch rats, an important job since a single rat would eat around 50 kilograms/110 pounds of food in its three-year life. Initial scepticism among farmers, which Talbot described as 'stiff old English prejudices – stiff as the Kentish clay', slowly evaporated as the girls showed their worth.

Endless queues

By the winter of 1917, queues for food became a dreary daily routine. The press reported on the 3,000 Londoners, six abreast, mostly women and children, waiting in icy December fog to buy margarine. People who worked out of shop hours could not get to the queues at all. In Walsall, Wolverhampton, 7,000 miners threatened to down tools, declaring that 'they could work at any time. What they needed now was food.' Resentment was shown to those who could afford to buy on the black market, or send out their servants to queue in their place.

Inevitably some went hungry. The government had been made aware of malnutrition among the ranks when recruiting soldiers in 1899 for the second Boer War. They found that the working class youth of the country were undernourished, suffering from rickets and of small stature. To get the numbers they needed, they had to reduce the minimum height for servicemen from 1.6 metres/5 feet 3 inches to 1.5 metres/5 feet.

## Rationing

Even though the Ministry of Food had been established in 1916 in order to 'promote economy and to maintain the food supply', it was not until February 1917 and the U-boat campaign that Lord Devonport, in his role as food controller, announced voluntary rationing. He would not make it compulsory, he said, as that would involve 'very elaborate machinery'. He concluded that 'a voluntary system is preferable until further experience is gained, and to meanwhile rely on the nation's instinct of self-discipline.' Heads of families should limit themselves to weekly purchases of 1.8 kilograms/4 pounds of bread, 1 kilogram/2.5 pounds of meat and 350 grams/12 ounces of sugar per person. Devonport appealed for everyone to eat less, particularly to eat less bread. It became a criminal offence to throw rice at weddings, or to adopt or feed stray dogs. Luxury chocolates and sweets were banned. Horses, cows and even pigeons were put on rations. Bread and cake sold in shops was reduced to 55 grams/2 ounces per person. The only bread permitted was government regulation bread, which was now mixed with barley or other grains. The message was to 'eat slowly' and 'keep warm', so as to need less food – a tall order, since coal was rationed too. Many, however, kept their sense of humour against the odds:

> How does the little busy wife,
> Improve the shining hour.
> She shops and cooks and works all day,
> The best within her power.
> How carefully she cuts the bread.
> How thin she spreads the jam.
> That's all she has for breakfast now,
> Instead of eggs and ham.
> (Anonymous spoof of 'Against Idleness and Mischief'
> by Isaac Watts)

As voluntary rationing did not catch on, more rigorous measures were put in place by the new food controller, Lord Rhondda. From January 1918 sugar was rationed, followed over the next four months by meat, butter, cheese and margarine. Ration cards were issued and everyone had to register with a butcher and grocer, which inspired one anonymous scribe to adapt the nursery bedtime prayer:

> Mathew, Mark, Luke and John,
> Guard the dish the butter's on
> For we don't want a theft.
> Four coupons I have left
> One for sugar, one for fat
> And two for liver for the cat.

Don't tell DORA 'bout the puss
Or she'll make an awful fuss.

The situation gradually improved after the introduction of the naval convoys to protect merchant ships, and rationing brought the much-hated queues down.

## How digging for DORA helped the war effort

When, in June 1917, there was such a shortage of potatoes that the government ordered hotels to serve them only on Tuesdays and Fridays, the allotment potato crop harvested that year made a considerable difference, and brought prices down. Gerald Butcher of the VLCS was triumphant, saying it was their greatest achievement ever. He rejoiced that 'In the veins of every Englishman runs the blood of the old-time yeoman of the soil.' Churches joined the thanksgiving with outdoor services in which the congregation would walk around the church, the plot-holders bearing their gardening tools in procession behind the choir.

**Seeing the funny side** A writer for the *Spectator* threw this light on the allotmenteer's wartime contribution: 'Although the "allottee" may be convinced in his own breast of the vital importance of allotments, nothing of this conviction is allowed to be seen. In the first instance, of course, this is due to the fact that we are British. Nothing will induce the normal Briton to do otherwise than minimize his deeds, from rushing a German pill-box to raising twenty hundredweight of good sound potatoes.' The article goes on to reveal the 'food for laughter' provided by an allotment: 'Cabbages **Seeing the funny side** are funny things. Lewis Carroll knew it (see page 209). W. S. Gilbert saw the humour of a French bean. And what is more ridiculous than an onion? ... The "cabbage patch", whether of ten rods or ten acres, can never attain to dignity. But if the allotment-holder laughs at his allotment, he does not want to lose it.'

In July 1918, the king and queen, accompanied by Rowland Prothero, president of the Board of Agriculture, were filmed by Pathé News visiting some south London allotments – Putney Lower

Common, Wimbledon Park Piggeries and Allotments, London South Western Railway Power Station Allotments, Merton Park Allotments, Ridgeway Place Allotments, Wimbledon, rounding off at Tooting and Battersea Rise. Much praise was lavished on the plot holders by the royal party.

When the war ended in November 1918, allotments were in full swing. In little more than eighteen months since the Dig for DORA campaign had been launched, the number of plots had tripled from some half a million to 1.5 million. Allotment societies were now organized and formed into associations or federations, grouped in turn under the new National Union of Allotment Holders. The NUAH was furthermore linked to the Cooperative Union and the Distributive Union of Cooperative Stores. This arrangement benefited the growers by giving them access to cheap tools and gardening necessities, as well as an outlet for the sale of surplus produce.

**1.5 million allotments**

Gerald Butcher was justifiably proud of the way the British people had risen to the occasion. Looking back in 1918, he recorded with satisfaction that allotment holders had 'rendered magnificent service', and in no small measure 'added to the food supply at a time when a grave shortage was imminent'. Allotment-grown produce meant 'that within a few weeks the wretched potato queues were abolished' and 'the consumption of bread was markedly reduced, enormous quantities of meat and other foodstuffs were saved, as also were transport and labour.' All this was 'of inestimable advantage to the country'.

Demand for allotments continued unabated after the war. This was partly due to a steep rise in the price of food, mass demobilization, closure of the munitions factories and the reclamation of war-time plots. Britain was now undoubtedly a nation of growers. This was just as well. Hard times lay ahead as the Depression loomed.

# 10. THE DEPRESSION, THE QUAKERS & ALLOTMENTS FOR THE MINERS 1918–1939

'The allotment scheme is the best thing devised yet,
for it definitely gives a man a chance to prove
whether he is likely to make good on a permanent land scheme.
It is only a stepping stone, I know, but it is
a stepping stone out of Slough and Despond.'

*S. P. B. Mais (1933)*

When the guns finally fell silent on 11 November 1918 and bells of victory rang across the country, Britain had become a remarkably more democratic place than it had been before the war. In 1918 all men over twenty-one were enfranchised, and all women over thirty. Ten years later, the age for women was lowered to twenty-one. In 1924, the first Labour government came in under Ramsay MacDonald – the illegitimate son of a Scottish labourer and a housemaid. This was more than 'dishing the dukes'. It was history in the making. While waiting for an audience with the king, John Robert Clynes, the Oldham-born son of an illiterate Irish labourer, and future home secretary, was heard to remark of himself and his cabinet colleagues: 'MacDonald the starveling clerk, Thomas the engine-driver, Henderson the foundry labourer, and Clynes the mill-hand, all to this pinnacle!'

**Homes fit for heroes** Britain emerged from the war heavily in debt. A brief boom in 1919, with a burst of shipbuilding, was all too soon followed by bust in the 1920s. There was also an acute housing shortage as all building of private houses had ceased during the war. Lloyd George

1920s postcard of an allotment holder proudly showing his onions.

promised in 1918 to create a land fit for heroes, with half a million new homes. After a triumphant start, which included the creation of the largest council estate in the world – 27,000 houses at the Becontree estate in Dagenham – the plan was ditched due to lack of funds.

By 1921 there were 2 million unemployed – 11.3 per cent of the working population. The most distressed areas were the industrial heartlands of South Wales, West Scotland, Lancashire, Tyneside and West Yorkshire, where unemployment rose to 80 per cent in some places. The government capped working hours and prohibited overtime. Women gave up their wartime jobs for the men. The demand for allotments shot up.

**Rising unemployment**

## Owners reclaim wartime allotments

In December 1918, just a few weeks after the armistice, local authorities provided land for an extra 5,000 allotments. Yet throughout 1919 there were around 7,000 applications for council allotments every week. Some sites divided the 10-pole (250-square metre) plots up into smaller units to spread them further. Another government initiative, the 1919 Land Settlement Act, was passed to set up war veterans as smallholders. The plan was to provide them with land on credit to be repaid over sixty years. Some 84,000 hectares/208,000 acres were bought on this plan within two years, before the scheme collapsed.

**Everyman's allotments** An article in the *Spectator* entitled 'Speed the Plough' backed the cause for more allotments: 'A good many holders of allotments find that their tenancy is coming to an end, and there is a disposition to regard their labour as a kind of war service which need not be repeated. This is a great mistake. The work of allotment-holders should not only be continued but expanded.' The article predicted that in the period of scarcity to come, 'the products of allotments and small gardens may make all the difference in countless families between comfort and want ... Potatoes may disappear from Covent Garden because the government try to interfere with economic laws, but the man who has just lifted two or three hundredweight of potatoes from his back garden or his allotment and placed them in a dry shed can afford to smile.'

The Board of Agriculture decided to extend the wartime tenancies created under DORA (see page 147) until the harvest of 1920. In spite of this measure, the number of allotments dropped as private wartime sites were gradually returned to their owners, and some of the public parks – over which the Board of Agriculture had no jurisdiction – were reclaimed by the councils.

**Parks return to normal** The editor of *Amateur Gardening*, T. W. Sanders, regretted the decision of the London County Council 'to withdraw the privilege of continuing the cultivation of allotments in their parks and recreation grounds at the end of 1919 ... as it will deprive hundreds, if not thousands of citizens from carrying out their patriotic efforts to grow food crops for the sustenance of themselves as well as their families.' (*Allotment and Kitchen Gardens*) By 1920, the number of plots had fallen 170,000 below their peak of 1.5 million at the end of the war.

## Security of tenure & the Allotments Act of 1922

Without any guarantees for security of tenure, many allotment holders were unwilling to commit themselves to the responsibilities of keeping a plot. Complaints began to reach the government about allotment land being taken by local councils ostensibly for essential building, but then left standing vacant. In response to these accusations, the Ministry of Agriculture requested that councils use the powers given them in the 1908 Small Holdings and Allotments Act to acquire more land through compulsory purchases, or at least to rent land that they could then let out as plots. The ministry made it clear that building contractors did not have the right to evict tenants on statutory allotments without the backing of the council.

The Ministry of Agriculture acknowledged the problem of tenure in a 1922 issue of its journal, pointing out that it had 'hitherto been one of the chief grievances of allotment holders that they were liable to be dispossessed of their plots on short notice.' Although allotment holders were entitled by law to compensation for crops if evicted, the Ministry of Agriculture argued that this fell short of meeting their contention. Having put 'a considerable amount of time and labour into the cultivation of their plots, they were liable to be dispossessed without being able to reap the full reward of their labours.'

The Allotments Act of 1922 provided some security for plot holders by imposing a six-month notice to quit. If there was urgent need to build, though, three would suffice. Compensation was increased. Plots were limited to 0.1 hectares/0.25 acres, this being calculated to supply enough vegetables for a family of four. The act prohibited commerce and defined allotments (as they are still defined today) as an area 'not exceeding forty poles in extent which is wholly or mainly cultivated by the occupier for the production of vegetable or fruit crops for consumption by himself or his family.' That put a stop to the common practice of growing flowers for sale.

**1922 Allotments Act**

In 1925 a key clause to protect allotments – one of the vital threads upon which the future of allotments still hang – was introduced. It ruled that any ground purchased by a local authority

**Key clause**

for allotments (making them 'statutory') could not be converted to other use or sold without ministerial permission.

In 1923 an Allotments Advisory Committee was established to guide the Ministry of Agriculture on allotment matters in England and Wales. The following year, the Agricultural Organization Society (AOS) decided that, as the farming side was now well covered by the National Farmers' Union and the ministry, it would drop agriculture and specialize in allotments and smallholdings. Keeping the same initials, it became the Allotment Organization Society. In 1930, the AOS, Small Holders Ltd. and the National Union of Allotment Holders were all absorbed into the new National Allotment Society.

## The miners, unemployment & the Society of Friends
During the Depression, the idea of providing allotments as a means to help the unemployed and keep up morale gained impetus in both the private and public sectors.

THE LEVER BREAKS.

Punch cartoon by Bernard Partridge showing the TUC, having called the 1926 General Strike, buckling under only nine days later, leaving the miners to struggle on alone.

Although the key **Coal** industries were in decline in the 1920s, coal still powered the country. George Orwell summed up its importance in his essay 'Down the Mine' (written in 1937, after his visit to a pit): 'In order that Hitler may march the goose-step, that the Pope may denounce Bolshevism, that the cricket crowds may assemble at Lords, that the poets may scratch one another's backs, coal has got to be forthcoming.' Orwell was appalled by the antiquated conditions, convinced that they would have killed him in a matter of days. 'Most of the things one imagines in hell are there – heat, noise, confusion, darkness, foul air, and, above all, unbearably cramped space,' he wrote, describing the 'half-naked kneeling men, one to every four or five yards, driving their shovels under the fallen coal and flinging it swiftly over their left shoulders'.

Winston Churchill, as Chancellor of the Exchequer in 1925, fixed sterling too high against the price of gold with dire consequences for the miners and the coal industry. As depicted by Matt, 1929.

In 1925 Chancellor Winston Churchill made a miscalculation with dire consequences for the miners. He fixed sterling against the price of gold too high for Britain to be competitive in the world market. As demand dropped, the pit owners called a slowdown in production, laid off men, cut wages by 13 per cent and increased working hours. When 1 million miners went on strike in May 1926, their slogan was 'Not a penny off the pay, not a second on the day'. The owners responded by locking them out over two days, following

Defeated miners returning to work. The pit owners only kept on the most skilled workers. *The Times* described the unemployed miners as '1,000,000 souls facing starvation'.

**General strike** which the Trades Union Congress (TUC) flexed its muscles and called a general strike across other industries – iron and steel, transport, the dockworkers and printers, as well as workers in the building, electrical and chemical trades.

There were fights between thousands of special police and strikers. The government sent a warship to Newcastle. The strikers derailed the Flying Scotsman. The Archbishop of Canterbury made an appeal for peace in the name of all the Christian churches. After nine days, Stanley Baldwin, the prime minister and a cool mediator, managed to persuade the TUC to call the strike off without making a single concession.

This left the miners to struggle on alone until hunger and despair drove them back to work. Within the year, the Trades Disputes Act banned sympathy strikes and mass picketing. **No concessions**

The pit owners kept on the most skilled workers and let the others go. Some would never work again. Many who owned their homes were not even eligible for unemployment benefit. *The Times* described the miners as '1,000,000 souls facing starvation', and another witness recounted how 'crowds of miners sitting on their heels was a sight never to be forgotten.'

During the strike, the Quaker Society of Friends (SOF) had met with the mine workers' leaders, the TUC and the coal owners. Now they decided to step in to help the miners body and soul. Through the newly formed Coalfields Distress Committee, they raised money for food and clothes, and provided canteens to feed thousands of miners. The SOF also tried to raise morale by providing mending work for the women and training the men to repair boots. In South Wales they opened sixty-seven boot-repairing centres, where miners fixed more than 75,000 boots in 1926.

The SOF set up permanent premises at Maes-yr-haf, in Glamorgan, to organize work training clubs for the young men, many of whom were homeless and sleeping rough. Sent out to restore playing fields, cricket grounds and roads, they were paid a trade-union rate and were given a hot meal. By 1927, membership reached 2,397. Most of the men managed to find employment through the scheme or by joining the government training centres.

Following the Wall Street Crash in 1929, Britain's already beleaguered world trade dropped again by half. Heavy industry – coal, steel and iron – fell by a third. Unemployment reached 3.5 million, with thousands more only able to get part-time jobs. Building on its experience with the unemployed, in 1930 the SOF closed down its Coalfields Distress Committee to concentrate on allotments for the deprived mining areas in Wales, Durham and Yorkshire. Its work was assisted by a fresh grant of £15,000 from the Lord Mayor of London's Fund. Seed potatoes, fertilizer, lime and tools were purchased and sold on to allotment holders at half the cost **Wall Street Crash** price. Some miners were slow to take up the offer, fearing that their unemployment benefit would be cut if they were caught gardening in the day. The National Union of Allotment Holders intervened and managed to get assurances that as long as the men were seen to make every effort to get work there would be no loss of benefits.

Impressed by the SOF's work, the government, under Ramsay MacDonald, decided to help. It set up twenty-five committees run by county officials, to provide supplies along the same lines as the SOF, and put in £42,833 for allotments for the unemployed in general. After a year's involvement, they had increased the number of plots from the SOF's total of 21,500 to 64,000, with the satisfying result of £400,000-worth of produce. As the *Journal of the Ministry of Agriculture* reported in 1933, without the scheme's supply of fresh vegetables many families would 'have to go short of such food'.

**Keeping hunger at bay**

The journal also commented approvingly: 'The idea has received support from all political parties, and there is no question of the beneficial results, both morally and physically, and the displays at various horticultural shows testify to the excellent results obtained by unemployed miners and other industrial workers.'

When the government dropped out of the project for lack of funds, the SOF galvanized itself once more. Joined by representatives of the Allotments Advisory Committee, their declared new aim was to enable 100,000 men to cultivate allotments for a year and 'help the unemployed to help themselves'. With this in mind, they ran a fund-raising poster campaign. *The Times* picked up the story in October 1932, saying that the 'obligation of all to succour the unemployed is stirring consciences everywhere ... From time to time there have been brought to public notice schemes to help men whose chronic lack of work is a physical and moral peril. One such scheme, which has abundantly proved its worth year after year, is that of the Society of Friends for providing allotments for unemployed or seriously impoverished people.' By 1933, the new SOF committee had also helped 100,000 unemployed men to get allotments on application to the town clerk. Inspired by this, 2,000 benevolent societies set up their own allotment schemes in the early 1930s.

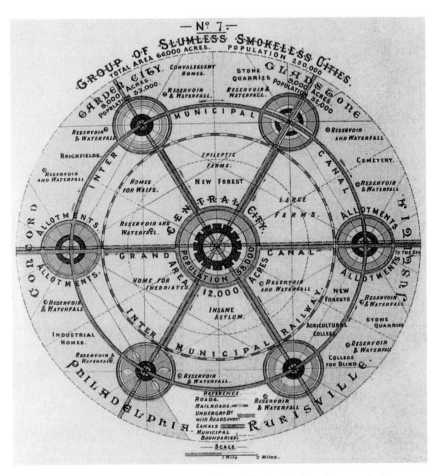

The Garden City concept. Ebenezer Howard's plan for 'slumless, smokeless cities' and which resulted in the new towns of Letchworth and Welwyn Garden City.

## Garden cities & the Land Settlement Association

Between the wars, there was a considerable drive to address the housing shortage, despite the sinking economy. Following the 1919 Housing and Town Planning Act, which made councils responsible for slum clearance and the provision of new housing, and after substantial government grants had been made to local authorities, just over

1 million council homes were built by 1939. The garden-city movement produced the new towns of Letchworth and Welwyn Garden City in Hertfordshire in the 1920s. They were founded by Ebenezer Howard, author of *Garden Cities of Tomorrow* (1898), whose utopian ideal was to combine the benefits of the city with those of the countryside.

**Metroland** Meanwhile, to the north-west of London, Metroland appeared as a ribbon development at the end of the Metropolitan Line. Looking to promote healthier living outside the city, the government also encouraged the private sector to get building. In 1919 the Ministry of Health produced its *Housing Manual* – a pattern book of simple housing designs. Entrepreneurial builders put up 4 million dwellings. These were largely semi-detached suburban houses with gabled front doors. They were built twelve to an acre (0.4 hectares), with sizeable back gardens that would earn their keep in the Second World War.

**Land Settlement Association** The Land Settlement Association, set up by the government in partnership with charities, turned its attention to resettling unemployed workers from the depressed industrial areas of the North-West and Wales. This scheme provided selected applicants with a cottage, 2 hectares/5 acres of land and some livestock. As with the Chartist Cooperative Land Society of the mid-nineteenth century, the plan was to create a cooperative of market gardens. Over a period of five years, 1,100 smallholdings were created in twenty-six settlements. A number flourished, but others failed as some of the townspeople did not adjust well to the hardships and low pay of farming life. The scheme was suspended in 1939.

## Allotments told to smarten up

During the Depression allotments began to be taken for granted by some and neglected – a problem that endures to this day.

**Blots on the landscape** A common complaint made by local residents concerned the unsightly huts and general mess on allotment sites. An article in *The Times* described plots swamped with tin cans, old baths and iron bedsteads. In contrast to this, however, the BBC broadcaster S.P.B. Mais (who started Radio 4's *Letter from America*) mentioned the care shown in Sheffield, where 'no fewer than 1,800 allotments have been taken by cutlers, moulders, razor makers, butcher's knife makers, fish hawkers, men in file trades, on gun lathes and colliers. The Sheffield men take special pride in hut construction and they use the huts in hot weather as their summer country houses. As they are on a bleak moorside they use them in winter to keep warm in the dinner hour.'

In 1936, the Ministry of Agriculture suggested that all public parks should have a model demonstration plot to promote higher standards. A booklet of useful tips was produced, which included a section on shed building. John Stoney, horticultural superintendent for Staffordshire, commented on the deplorable state of some huts and suggested hiding them with latticework or climbers. The government gave out about 400 grants of £10,000 for community huts. This only supplied one-sixth of allotments, but it was hoped that it would encourage others to sharpen up.

On 3 September 1939, the very day that Britain declared war on Germany, the British liner *Athenia* was torpedoed by a submarine. History was about to repeat itself. As in 1917, Germany would be aiming to starve Britain into submission by cutting off food supplies arriving by sea. In his memoirs, Churchill confessed that the only thing that ever really frightened him during the war was the 'U-boat peril'. Farming output would become a fight for the country's survival for the next six years. The farmers would strive to feed the nation at large as best they could and the public would help to feed themselves. Allotments, still well established with around 815,000 plots at the outbreak of war, and three-quarters of them in towns, were to be given a huge boost. Allotment heyday was about to arrive.

# 11. DIGGING FOR VICTORY 1939–1945

'It is clearly our duty, just as it is a matter
of elementary wisdom, to try to make doubly and trebly
sure that we will fight and win this war on full stomachs.
To do this we want not only the big man with the plough,
but the little man with the spade to get busy this autumn.'
*Sir Reginald Dorman-Smith (October 1939)*

The Allies were so war-weary that they failed to retaliate as Hitler, Germany's chancellor from 1933, repeatedly flouted the 1919 Treaty of Versailles. He rearmed, making alliances with Italy and Japan, and reoccupied both the Rhineland and Austria. When he demanded that the pro-Nazi Sudetenland region of northern Czechoslovakia be returned to Germany, it was conceded to him by France, Britain and Italy, who signed the Munich Agreement in September 1938.

Declaring that the agreement was a worthless piece of paper, Hitler invaded the rest of Czechoslovakia in March 1939. Britain and France had to act. They finally warned Germany that if Poland were invaded as well, there would be war. Having concluded the Molotov-Ribbentrop Pact with the Soviet Union at the end of August, to slice up Poland between them, Hitler attacked Poland on 1 September. Two days later, Britain and France were at war with Germany.

On 6 September 1939, an editorial in the *Evening Standard* spoke of the spade being as mighty as the sword. This phrase to spur on the war effort was coined not by a governmental pundit but by a young Fleet Street journalist named Michael Foot (leader of the Opposition in the 1980s). 'Britain must learn to dig', wrote Foot.

'Not only must we dig in the cities. Every spare half acre from the Shetlands to the Scillies must feel the shear of the spade.' Referring to the 'Nazi raiders who will search for our food ships beneath the seas', he urged readers to remember that 'food wins victories as surely as gunpowder ... By husbanding our food resources, by searching out new soil from which to add to our stores, we may contribute perhaps decisively to the finish of this contest. Tell your neighbour and remember yourself that the order is to dig. The spade may prove as mighty as the sword.'

**The shear of the spade**

Little progress had been made on self-sufficiency in the British Isles since the Great War. In 1939 one-third of the nation's food, including 90 per cent of wheat, was still being imported.

The German U-boats, now grouping around their targets in lethal wolf packs of fifteen to twenty, would sink 2,400 British cargo ships by 1945. Around 30,000 merchant navy men would lose their lives in the course of the Battle of the Atlantic.

**Wolf packs**

Reporting on losses to British shipping in the first week of the war, and comparing this figure to the even greater losses in 1917, Michael Foot wrote: 'Our Navy will smite back and reduce the total, just as it did in that earlier contest. But the submarine can be defeated on every square foot of British soil as well as on the high seas. So the order which the *Evening Standard* gave a week ago must be rammed home: Dig for Victory.' These three words provided the famous slogan at the heart of a propaganda campaign the like of which had never been seen before. All means available – posters, radio broadcasts, newspapers, cinema – were used to get the nation digging for victory.

Government scientists had calculated that 40.5 hectares/ 100 acres of potatoes could feed 400 people for a year. The same acreage of oats would feed 170, whereas beef would feed only nine. They decided to plough up 809,000 hectares/ 2 million acres of pasture, replacing it with potatoes and corn before winter – something of a challenge, as it was already September.

**Oats & Potatoes**

Remarkably, the goal was achieved on time. A vast extent of new arable land was sown with winter and spring crops – though not without considerable effort. Retired cart horses were put back into harness. Disused ploughs were patched up by blacksmiths. Shepherds, stockmen and other vital farm workers were held back from signing up so they could carry out 'essential services'. Farmers worked by moonlight, both then and throughout the war.

The British agricultural sector had already been put on a formal war footing two days before war was declared. Telegrams had been sent out to the 'War Ags' Committees, established originally during the First World War and now reassembled ahead of time (see page 153). They were given an overall target for land reclamation and further targets for different types of crop.

**Land reclamation**

They had powers to take possession of inefficient farms, also to give out grants and supply equipment. They organized mobile crews and machinery as a way of combatting the shortage of tractors. To supply this massive operation with essential information, the biggest national farm survey since the Domesday Book of 1086 was undertaken by volunteers, recording every farm of more than 2 hectares/5 acres.

Countrywide reclamation using industrial machinery was to leave its mark permanently on the landscape. Some 243,000 hectares/ 600,000 acres would have been ploughed up by the end of the war, including thousands of acres in the Welsh mountains. The Norfolk fens were drained. In Wiltshire, 202 hectares/500 acres of King's Heath – granted to the commoners in the tenth century by King Athelstan – were churned over.

**The fall of France**

Following months of uneasy waiting during the phoney war, France was invaded and capitulated to Germany in June 1940.

Britain, although by now well prepared, was suddenly alone in facing the enemy. Winston Churchill, who had taken over from Neville Chamberlain in May that year, informed his Cabinet that he had 'nothing to offer but blood, toil, tears and sweat'. Speaking in the House of Commons the following month, he declared: 'The Battle of France is over. I expect that the Battle of Britain is about to begin.'

Next came the Blitz. In the nightly 'terror attacks', more than 1 million houses were bombed in London and some 20,000 civilians

In 1939, 809,000 hectares/2 million acres of pasture were dug up and replaced with potatoes and corn in the first few months of the war in a massive drive to feed the nation.

killed, accounting for half the national total of civilian deaths. In Liverpool, another prime target because of its port, 4,000 people died. Northern industrial cities with munitions, tank and Spitfire factories were heavily damaged. Coventry was practically wiped out. Churchill commented: 'The British nation is unique in this respect. They are the only people who like to be told how bad things are, who like to be told the worst, and like to be told that they are very likely to get much worse in the future and must prepare themselves for further reverses.'

## We need more allotments

City-dwellers were prevailed upon to get digging. 'Half a million more allotments properly worked will provide potatoes and vegetables that will feed another million adults and one and a half million children for eight months out of twelve. The matter is not one that can wait. So – let's get going. Let "Dig for Victory" be the motto of everyone with a garden and of every able-bodied man and woman capable of digging an allotment in their spare time.' Those were the words of Sir Reginald Dorman-Smith, Minister of Agriculture, when launching the Dig for Victory campaign in a radio broadcast on 3 October 1939.

**Dig for Victory**

There were 815,000 allotment plots in Britain at the start of the war. In addition, there were some 3.5 million private gardens, including the new back gardens of dwellings built in the housing boom that followed the Great War (see page 160). The goal set by Professor John Raeburn, an agricultural economist and statistician at the newly reinstated Ministry of Food, was to increase the number of allotments by more than half, bringing the total back up to the 1920s peak of just over 1.3 million plots.

Railway sidings, tennis courts, golf courses, grass verges, playing fields and school playgrounds were turned over to allotments. The London parks put 34 hectares/83 acres down to oats and root crops, and a further 25 hectares/63 acres to allotments. The gardens of museums and palaces – even Aintree Racecourse – were ploughed up. Windsor Great Park was said to be the largest wheat field in the

# "Dig for Victory"

— SAYS THE MINISTER OF AGRICULTURE —

"LET this be the slogan of every one with a garden : of every able-bodied man and woman capable of digging an allotment in their spare time.

"In war we must make every effort. All the potatoes, all the cabbages, and all the other vegetables, we can produce may be needed. That is why I appeal to you, lovers of this great country of ours, to dig, to cultivate, to sow, and to plant.

"Our fellow-countrymen in the Forces abroad and at home are playing their part. I am confident that you, equally, will do yours by producing the maximum food from gardens and allotments."

Plea signed by Reginald Dorman-Smith, minister of agriculture in 1939, for the country to get digging.

country, and there was a pig farm in Hyde Park. As in the previous war, vegetables were grown in the grounds of Buckingham Palace, and there were allotments around the Albert Memorial and in Kensington Gardens. More sprung up in the quads of Oxford and Cambridge colleges, on the Fellows' Lawn at London Zoo and in the dry moat of the Tower of London, as well as in churchyards and bomb sites.

Vegetables thrived in window boxes, on the roof gardens of hotels and department stores, and on top of Anderson shelters. These were named after John Anderson, the man in charge of air-raid preparations. They were made out of sheets of corrugated iron bolted together, with steel plates at either end and an earthen blast door.

**Marrows on the roof**

They were half-buried and covered with a minimum of 38 centimetres/ 15 inches of soil for further protection and camouflage – ideal for sun-loving vegetables like marrows. On occasion there were competitions among neighbours for the best-planted shelter roof.

Once more land had been freed up, the next step for the Ministry of Food was to teach people how to grow. Since many new allotment holders had no experience of gardening, the ministry used every possible means to provide them with help and information. Week-long Dig for Victory events with popular personalities went on tour, as did a travelling exhibition with information sheets provided by the Royal Horticultural Society (RHS). The society also supplied local lecturers with lantern slides. The RHS's *Vegetable Garden Displayed*, first published in 1941, was its most successful book ever and is still in print today.

**Stream of advice** The national press jumped on the bandwagon. *The Times*, the *Daily Mirror* and *Daily Mail* ran gardening articles. Periodicals with advice on wartime growing included the *Gardeners' Chronicle, Home Gardening, Amateur Gardening* and *My Garden*, as well as women's magazines such as *Woman* and *Good Housekeeping*.

Also popular were the Ministry of Food's own *Grow More Food* booklets, priced at 3d or 4d each. Topics included food and preserves from the garden, how to cultivate tomatoes, and wartime poultry keeping. The first bulletin, 'Grow for Winter as well as Summer', contained an unfortunate printing error – it recommended that marrows be sown 3 inches (7.5 centimetres) rather than 3 feet (90 centimetres) apart. Despite this embarrassing start, the ministry went on to provide excellent advice under the new *Dig For Victory* title. This series of twenty-six free leaflets covered everything from home-made Bordeaux mixture to storing potatoes for seed. *How to Plan a 5-pole Plot*, with an application form tucked inside it, was published to accompany the smaller plots introduced when the government saw that an allotment of 10 poles (253 square metres/303 square yards) was too much for busy people. In 1945 came the ministry's last series, practical month-by-month *Allotment and Garden Guides*.

**Awards & encouragement** To encourage further diligence, the Ministry of Agriculture set up a reward scheme for plots judged 'best cultivated to produce a continuous supply of the most suitable vegetables throughout the year'. Out of 10,000 applications, 4,000 people won signed certificates of merit. Further encouragement was handed out with signs that gardeners could display to announce that theirs was a 'Victory Garden'.

## Rationing & fair shares all round

Despite every effort by farmers and allotmenteers, in January 1940 rationing was brought in. A few months later, Lord Woolton was appointed to take the helm at the Ministry of Food. It was

A Ministry of Food poster teaching the public how to grow food all year round on an allotment.

an inspired choice. Born Frederick Marquis, a grammar-school boy from Salford, Lancashire, his single-minded mission was to defeat poverty and malnutrition, especially in children. He had moved on from an economics research fellowship at Manchester University to later become director at the employee-owned Lewis's department store in Liverpool. In 1939 he served as adviser to the secretary of state for war and was given a peerage for services to industry.

**Uncle Fred**      An avuncular figure, he became known affectionately to the nation at large as 'Uncle Fred' and was often addressed as such in correspondence.

Woolton was advised on rationing by specialists including Professor Jack Drummond, biochemist and author of *The Englishman's Food: A History of Five Centuries of English Diet* (1939), and Boyd Orr, a Scottish teacher, doctor and research scientist. As an undergraduate in Glasgow, Orr had witnessed the effects of poverty in the slums. While serving as medical officer to an infantry unit, the Sherwood Foresters, in the First World War, he attended the wounded in the trenches and was awarded the Military Cross at the Battle of the Somme. He insisted that the troops got fresh vegetables collected from local gardens. In 1918 Orr worked for the Royal Society on the allocation of food resources before returning to his post as director of Aberdeen University's institute of nutrition. In *Food, Health and Income* (1936), he concluded that more than half the population lacked the resources for a good diet and 10 per cent were severely undernourished.

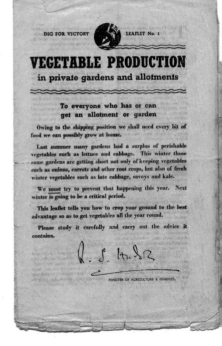

Introductory note by Robert Hudson, minister of Agriculture and Fisheries from 1940–1945, on Dig for Victory Leaflet no 1 for private gardens and allotments with advice on a cropping plan, storage, soil and potato blight.

The war saw a boom in gardening education for the public in books, articles, radio broadcasts, demonstrations and government leaflets.

Woolton was to recall in his memoirs that he and his advisers 'worked out a diet for the nation that would supply all the calories and all the vitamins that were needed for the different age groups, for the fighting services, for the heavy manual workers, for the ordinary housewife, for the babies and the children, and for pregnant and nursing mothers.' There would be 'fair shares all round'. Trade brands of staple foods were replaced by a single national **The war** brand – most famously, the leaden war loaf, sold a day late to **loaf** make it even less appetizing and so last longer.

Standard rations included a weekly allowance of 340 grams/ 12 ounces each of sugar and margarine, 225 grams/8 ounces of cheese, 110 grams/4 ounces each of tea and bacon (or ham), 85 grams/3 ounces of lard and 1/2d-worth of meat (just over 450 grams/1 pound). To this were added 450 grams/1 pound of jam and sweets per month, and either one egg a week or a packet of egg powder each month. By 1941, the rations were squeezed to half of this.

Special allowances were made for particular needs, such as those of invalids. Vegetarians had extra eggs and cheese. Members of the armed services and miners were entitled to larger portions. Children under five were given free orange juice and cod liver oil as part of the Welfare Food Scheme, introduced to protect their health during rationing.

If an alternative 'basal' diet had been accepted, rationing could have taken an even blander form. Churchill, however, vetoed it outright. 'The way to lose the war', he told Lord Woolton, 'is to force the British public into a diet of milk, oatmeal, potatoes etc., washed down on gala occasions with a little lime juice.'

## The Kitchen Front

To help the public with the challenges of rationing, the Ministry of Food provided recipes in the form of 'Food Flashes' at the cinema. An important source of public information, the cinemas on every high street regularly showed Pathé newsreels and sold 25–30 million tickets each week during the war. Similarly, government issue 'Food Facts' appeared in newspapers and magazines. Radio provided another channel, even though all regional stations had been blocked the day before war broke out and replaced by the BBC Home Service.

**Gert & Daisy** The popular comedy duo, Gert and Daisy, were given prime airtime every day after the 8a.m. news to broadcast cheerily on *The Kitchen Front*. Home economist Marguerite Patten taught every cook in Britain to behave 'like a zealous squirrel' and gave out wartime recipes such as the 'Woolton Pie' devised by the Savoy's head chef. It was made with root vegetables, 'thickened vegetable water' and potato-flour pastry.

Lord Woolton's voice was generally only heard when there was a change for the worse to announce. His talks were carefully prepared with the 'ordinary man at home firmly in his sights', and were well received despite the ever-more gloomy news on rationing. Waste was severely discouraged, even punished. Woolton pointed out that the result of each person wasting just half an ounce (14 grams) of bread per day for a year would be a mountain weighing 250,000 tons, or enough cargo to fill thirty wheat ships. The home cook was prevailed upon to be frugal:

'Those who have the will to win,
Cook potatoes in their skin,
Knowing that the sight of peelings,
Deeply hurts Lord Woolton's feelings.'

This verse appeared as part of a campaign to encourage people to eat potatoes instead of bread. Recipe books, posters, advertisements and radio jingles appeared in the name of Potato Pete, a cartoon character created to get the message across. The popular entertainer Betty Driver (subsequently Betty Turpin in *Coronation Street*) provided the voice for the Potato Pete anthem, and traditional nursery rhymes were also adapted to the theme:

'There was an old woman who lived in a shoe.
She had so many children she didn't know what to do.
She gave them potatoes instead of some bread,
And the children were happy and very well fed.'

An unexpected surplus of 100,000 tons of carrots led to the invention of another vegetable character, Dr Carrot, whose family members (Carroty George, Pop and Clara Carrot) were designed by Walt Disney at Lord Woolton's request. In the hope of hoodwinking the Germans, it was even put about that Royal Air Force (RAF) pilots – who were in fact now equipped with radar – had magically developed night vision by eating carrots. Posters read 'Night sight can mean life or death.' Mrs Hudson, when appearing on the radio programme *The Kitchen Front* in 1941, informed her listeners that the vitamin A in carrots 'strengthens our eyes so we can adjust them quickly to the dark. Good blackout food, you might say, and now that double daylight saving comes to an end, we'd be wise to eat more of them.'

To lessen the tedium of a limited diet and escape the horrors of dishes like 'stuffed ear' and 'melt and skirt pudding', Lord Woolton encouraged the population to eat out. Restaurants were ration-free. In addition, over 2,000 not-for-profit British Restaurants

(BRs) were set up nationwide. The original name suggested for them had been Communal Feeding Centres, but Churchill vetoed that as 'suggestive of communism and the workhouse'. In 1943 alone the BRs served 600,000 subsidized meals every day – at less than 9d for three courses. The Women's Voluntary Service (WVS) in their Harris tweed uniforms and pork pie hats designed by Norman Hartnell, the queen's couturier, pitched in as volunteers.

## Tuning in to Mr Middleton

'These are critical times,' said Cecil Henry Middleton, the famous wireless gardener, 'but we shall get through them, and the harder we dig for victory the sooner will the roses be with us.' Known affectionately as 'Mr' Middleton, he won the hearts of three-and-a-half million listeners, who tuned in to the BBC's *In Your Garden* on Sundays. Rather patronizingly, Wilfred Rooke Ley of the *Catholic Herald* described Middleton's ability to 'address himself to the lowest common denominator of horticultural intelligence without the faintest hint of superiority or condescension'.

The son of Sir George Sitwell's gardener, Middleton was brought up at Weston–by–Weedon in Northamptonshire. His first job, at age thirteen, was as garden boy at Weston Hall. After working for a London seed company, he moved on to train at the Royal Botanic Gardens, Kew. When the First World War war broke out he was working at the Board of Agriculture, and later taught horticulture for Surrey County Council. Then he was recommended to the BBC. Having tried out grandees such as Vita Sackville-West and the novelist Marion Cran (author of *The Garden of Ignorance* and *Making the Dovecote Pay*), the BBC was looking for a more down-to-earth broadcaster. The unassuming Mr Middleton fitted the bill perfectly. He aired his first talk in 1931 and began *In Your Garden* in 1934.

*In Your Garden*

In the preface to his book *Digging for Victory: Wartime Gardening with Mr Middleton* (1942), he recalled happier days when 'we talked about rock gardens, herbaceous borders, and verdant lawns; but with the advent of war and its grim demands, these pleasant features rapidly receded into the background to make way for the all-important food crops.' He felt that interest in gardening had been 'intensified by the urgent necessity of growing food', and hoped that his audience enjoyed him holding forth 'on leeks, lettuces and leatherjackets, instead of lilac, lilies, and lavender'.

He did not rule out growing a few flowers, suggesting **A bit of** some simple annuals scattered and raked in to the odd corner **frivolity** could lift the spirits. Everyone deserved 'a day off Hitler'. He encouraged people to take part in their local horticultural show, 'complete with flags, jangles and wangles, a band, a few speeches, darts competitions, bowling for a pig and other sideshows'. Those who disapproved of such frivolity got short shrift. 'There will always be local Jeremiahs to throw cold water on every suggestion but do not heed them.' After all, shows were an opportunity to raise money for the Red Cross, and the prizes might be a useful gardening book or a tin of fertilizer.

Rival RAF units took part in competitions held at the RHS hall in Vincent Square, London. By 1943, 2,900 hectares/7,200 acres at RAF airfields had been turned over to growing vegetables, valued at £250,000. While 'soldier-gardeners' ran kitchen gardens in requisitioned manor houses, civilians of all ages were urged to lend a hand in every way possible.

At harvest time, factory and office workers from towns and **Harvest-time** cities would head off to 'farming holiday camp'. They slept in **holidays** tents or hostels, sometimes in schools or town halls, and were paid one shilling an hour for their work regardless of experience or age.

Schoolchildren would also help on farms during the holidays, while during term-time boys over ten got time off school to pitch in for pocket money. The *Gardeners' Chronicle* reported that 162 hectares/400 acres were being cultivated by children in the West Riding in 1942.

Cubs and Brownies were sent out to forage in the hedgerows **Foraging** for nuts, berries and crab apples. They gathered wild salads – dandelions, burdock, fungi and young nettles. With their mothers, they picked enough rose hips to supply all the young in the country with rose-hip syrup – 500 tons in 1943.

Poster from the 'Waste Not, Want Not' campaign to recycle everything possible. Bins were left out in the street to collect bones, scrap metal and paper to make 'planes, guns, ships and ammunition'.

All this was still not enough. In the endeavor to limit waste to a minimum, the art of recycling reached new heights. Bones were boiled down for glue used in aircraft manufacture, ground for fertilizer or made into glycerin for explosives.

The 'Waste Not, Want Not' campaign, which ran in cinemas, on billboards and in the press, urged people to save paper, rags, metal and rubber, and put them out on the street in bags for the council to collect. A Ministry of Food advertisement joined the dots:

> 'Because of the pail, the scraps were saved,
> Because of the scraps, the pigs were saved,
> Because of the pigs, the rations were saved,
> Because of the rations, the ships were saved,
> Because of the ships , the island was saved,
> Because of the island, the Empire was saved,
> And all because of the housewife's pail.'

## Sparrow pie & rabbit clubs

In parallel to the Dig for Victory campaign, people were encouraged to raise livestock at home. By-laws on keeping animals in gardens were relaxed. It now became 'a patriotic duty' to have bees, hens, geese and ducks. The quiet, non-flying Indian runner duck was particularly popular. Bird feed – buckwheat, sunflowers or maize – was home-grown and any surplus either shared or bartered. Poultry meal could only be obtained in exchange for fresh eggs. Goats were kept for milk and cheese.

By 1943 there were 3,000 registered rabbit clubs. One buck and three does could produce fifty-five rabbits a year, enough for a weekly family stew. A handy government booklet entitled *How to Keep Rabbits* encouraged people to join the national scheme to 'produce more rabbit meat, furs and wool for yourself and the nation'. It was only possible to get rabbit food, though, if half the offspring were handed over to the butcher. There was little sympathy for wild rabbits. It was calculated that nine rabbits consumed as much as

Official British photo entitled 'Where Nazis sowed death, a Londoner and his wife have sown life-giving vegetables in a London bomb crater.'

two sheep. Sparrows, too, were considered a pest by the Ministry of Agriculture, which described them as 'Hitler's feathered friend' and asked that they be destroyed 'ruthlessly'. Sparrow pie was proposed. Country dwellers had an advantage with game. Pheasants and partridge were abundant, as shooting for sport was banned.

**Backyard pigs**
The Small Pig Keeper's Council, which provided companies, mines and schools with information on how to set up cooperatives, negotiated with local authorities during the war for people to keep pigs in their backyards. They advised on all porcine matters, including proper care for pigs, which could not be slaughtered until they reached 45 kilograms/100 pounds, and then only by a registered slaughterer. Pig clubs could only keep a certain amount of the pork per family, and were obliged to sell the rest to approved butchers at wholesale prices.

## Vegetable gluts and other problems

As the war progressed, there was a shortage of manure for the amateur grower. Farmers had priority, and there were far fewer farm animals due to the switch to arable farming. There were still some horse-drawn carts in the towns and their droppings were prized. Children were sent out to collect them but were often thwarted by a 'dung bag' attached to the rear of the horse. It was another reason to keep animals of all sorts.

**Manure hard to come by**

Compost was recommended. People should ask their local councils when grass verges were to be mowed, and collect the cuttings for their compost heaps at home – even better, do the mowing themselves to save the council's time. Those living in coastal regions could collect seaweed to fertilize their potatoes. Gardeners were advised to make their own potash (previously imported from Germany or neighbouring countries) by burning wood under a layer of soil to avoid risk of detection during blackouts.

With fertilizers also in short supply, National Growmore was developed by George Monro & Sons under government sponsorship and introduced in 1942. Still on sale today, it is an all-round granular fertilizer with a 7:7:7 ratio for nitrogen, potassium and phosphate. Known at the time as an 'artificial' fertilizer, as it was inorganic, it was rationed to what was considered an adequate amount for a ten-pole allotment.

**National Growmore fertilizer**

In 1943 the National Allotment Society (NAS) drew the government's attention to the fact that substandard seed potatoes were being sold and should be regulated. In order to encourage plot holders, they also pressed for greater security of tenure but achieved little more than promises of compensation if tenants had to leave during the growing season. The 600 societies affiliated to the NAS in 1939 increased to 2,300 by 1941.

Dealing with gluts was another problem faced by the new population of gardeners. The Minister of Agriculture, Robert Hudson (who had replaced Sir Reginald Dorman-Smith in 1940) received many complaints on this subject.

He was keen to promote a 'planned succession' so that

**Cropping plans**

'surplus to the grower's own requirements is of non-perishable vegetables that can be stored in the winter months.' *The Times* commented in 1942 that 'At the present moment the public, after having been exhorted to "dig for victory", are shocked to hear that hundreds of tons of fresh vegetables are allowed to rot or are ploughed back into the ground because the grower cannot obtain a remunerative price or even sell them at any price, while high prices are being asked for them in the shops.'

Elizabeth Hess, agricultural adviser to the National Federation of Women's Institutes (NFWI) came up with a solution. Using a government grant awarded to the federation to encourage 'the best use, preservation and marketing of home-grown produce', Hess set up more than 5,000 preservation centres countrywide. These collected, sorted and distributed gluts in partnership with the National Allotment Society and the County Garden Produce Committees.

**Tons of jam** Canning machines were donated to the NFWI by women's organizations in the United States and Canada, in addition to 600 tons of sugar. Alongside other women's organizations, the federation produced a prodigious quantity of jams, preserves, and tinned fruits and vegetables – 1.4 million kilograms/3 million pounds of jam and 150 tons of tinned fruit were sent to hospitals and orphanages in the first year. The NFWI also set up stalls in villages and towns for women gardeners to sell their home-made produce.

**Pilfering & trespass** Another cause of distress to allotment holders was pilfering and vandalism. There was no spare wire to fence off allotment sites. As Robert Hudson explained, in the absence of fencing it 'may not be easy to define what an allotment is, but it is like an elephant – you recognize it when you see it. We want to make abundantly clear to the public at large that, for the period of the emergency, that ground is the property of the man that works it.' The 1943 regulations on Trespass on Growing Crops made pilfering, even of a few cabbages and onions, punishable by weeks of hard labour or a hefty fine. In Stratford, London, a man was fined £20 for stealing a single onion, plus ten shillings for trespass.

Although many women were growing produce in their own

gardens, they remained reluctant to take up allotments, still an all-male domain. Some councils began to run 'Women's Allotment Week' campaigns.

However, by 1943 there were still only 10,000 allotments held in the names of women out of more than a million plots. **Women's Allotment Week** This was despite the fact that 10 million women were registered for work, including thousands in Royal Ordnance factories, in civil defence, in hospitals or the ambulance corps. They worked in the forces. In the voluntary sector they were found in the Townswomen's Guilds and the Women's Institutes, the Salvation Army and the Red Cross. In the reactivated Women's Land Army (see page 155), 80,000 young women took on physically demanding agricultural jobs. The 6,000 'lumberjills' in the Timber Corps worked in forests to get timber for mosquito aircraft and mine sweeper ships. In Norfolk, one hundred women dug up the huge trunks of petrified bog oaks in the fens before they could be blown up with dynamite to clear the area for growing crops.

This light-hearted verse written by a female gardener at Kew appeared in *The Journal of the Kew Guild* in 1939:

'Now Adam was a gardener, and God who made him sees
That half a gardener's proper work is done upon his knees;
But with Adam gone to fight the foe and only home on leave
The proper one to kneel and plant and grow our food is – EVE!'

Nevertheless, it was not always conceded that Eve could manage the job entirely on her own. Posters encouraging women to take up allotments often pictured them working under the supervision of men. The magazine *Garden Work for Amateurs* suggested in one its 1941 issues: 'Provided that the initial digging and trenching is carried out by a member of the sterner sex, I can see no reason at all why a woman cannot run an allotment with the greatest success.'

In *Keep Fit in Wartime* (1940), Dr Harry Roberts recommended gardening for fitness, women included. Growing food, he says, is an 'exhortation to health as well as helpfulness', and gardening a hobby

Members of the Women's Land Army harvesting beets. There were 80,000
Land Girls by 1940, headed by the formidable Lady Denman. They
undertook heavy farming work.

'not for the young only but for people of both sexes, of all ages and of
every class'.

## Dig on for victory

The propaganda machine tried to reinvigorate the flagging war effort
with a new campaign under the banner of 'Dig on for Victory'. The
government encouraged people to 'Keep on pushing in the spade!'
Even so, between 1943 and 1948 the number of allotment plots
dropped by more than 200,000, falling to a total of some 1.1 million.

Despite food shortages, despite rationing (or perhaps because of it), at the end of the war the nation was fitter than before. Everyone had eaten plenty of fresh vegetables and received lots of advice on health. Free milk for all children, as well as free orange juice and cod liver oil for the under fives, along with school lunches, produced taller, stronger children. In 1942, the Beveridge Report had identified the five evils that beset the country – Want, Disease, Ignorance, Squalor and Idleness. William Beveridge's proposals for dealing with them would form the foundation of the Welfare State. In 1944, infant deaths in the first year were the lowest ever recorded.

**A healthier nation**

Mr Middleton wrote: 'What can be said of the Dig for Victory campaign so far? Has it produced the expected results? Broadly speaking, I think so. The country is definitely garden minded, but we still have a long way to go.' It was a magnificent effort.

In 1942 half the population took part in growing food, contributing 70 per cent of vegetables to the nation's diet. *The Times* estimated that the 40,000 hectares/100,000 acres of land occupied by allotments would amount to the area of Rutland, and with private gardens added in, it would include Huntingdonshire as well. At the height of wartime allotment fever, there had been more than 1.4 million plots producing over 1.3 million tons of vegetables a year – not far off one ton each. Four million families were growing their own vegetables.

**Accolades for the war efforts**

However, there was to be no slacking. The food situation would get worse before it got better, due, as Lord Woolton warned, 'to the urgent necessity of feeding the starving people of Europe'. Mr Middleton wrote in the *Daily Express* in May 1945, a fortnight after the Allied victory in Europe, that 'We may yet have to change 'Dig for Victory' into 'Dig for Dear Life.'

# 12. POST-WAR DOLDRUMS & THE GREEN REVOLUTION

'We advocate ambition, without which good practice
cannot be achieved, an ambition that encompasses allotment sites
which are fully tenanted, well appointed and well managed,
open to all, valued in many ways by the local authority
and the communities it serves, and with a secure future.'
Richard Wiltshire & Deborah Burn,
*Growing in the Community* (2008)

The years following the end of the Second World War brought little relief from hardship for the British population. Many who lived through it have said that they did not go hungry at the time, only afterwards. Yet despite the government's attempt to sustain Dig for Victory into peacetime, allotments went into free fall.

Half a million plots had vanished by 1947, mostly because the land was returned to its former use. That year brought an exceptionally bitter winter, followed by floods which destroyed much of the winter stores. As a result, not only were potatoes rationed until the following June, but many allotment growers simply lost heart.

**Welcome new law**  In 1950, the minister of agriculture, Tom Williams, introduced a new Allotment Act that required councils to give plot holders twelve months' notice to quit – a long-awaited extension. The National Allotment Society (by this time renamed the National Allotment and Garden Society, or NAGS) had been pressing for security of tenure throughout the war, but until now had been waved away with little more than vague promises of compensation. Despite the new law, however, uptake remained sluggish. Between 1950 and 1964, the number of plots dropped to

729,000. George W. Giles, general secretary of NAGS, seemed to be wringing his hands when he wrote to *The Times* in February 1952:

'I cannot understand why so many able-bodied men do not exercise their statutory right and obtain an allotment ... The National Allotment and Garden Society have a scheme where old-age pensioners, the disabled, the blind, widows and the unemployed can, thanks to charitable support from the public, obtain garden necessities at reduced rates and so gain the full benefit from their allotments. There is simply no reason why people should not start growing their own food and so help alleviate some of the pressure from the nation's overwrought economy.'

Rationing finally ended in 1952, seven years after peace was declared. At last, people were a little more affluent. There were cars on the road. The first supermarkets were making their way into Britain's high streets in the 1960s. Convenience food, in the form of sliced bread and frozen peas, had come in from America. **No more rations**

In 1965, the Ministry of Land and Resources set up a committee to investigate the decline in allotments. It was headed by Harry Thorpe, professor of geography at Birmingham University. A questionnaire was sent out to 900 urban councils and 8,500 parish councils (not altogether well received), and a different one to plot holders.

The Thorpe Report of 1969 advised a complete overhaul of allotment law. It **The Thorpe Report**

Professor Harry Thorpe, author of the 1969 *Thorpe Report,* proposed that allotments should be replaced by leisure gardens and that allotment law should be overhauled.

195

also proposed that allotments should be replaced by leisure gardens, as found in Germany, Denmark and the Netherlands. These would be landscaped, with surfaced roads for easy access, and facilities and communal buildings paid for by the plot holders. The report did not lead to any government action. However, the report's recommendation to provide fifteen full-sized (ten-pole or 250-square metre) plots per 1,000 households was widely adopted as a yardstick by local authorities.

The National Allotment and Garden Society added 'leisure gardens' to its title, possibly as a result of the Thorpe Report, becoming the National Society of Allotments and Leisure Gardeners (NSALG) – as it is today.

## Continuing decline

By 1970 a further fall in the number of plots brought the national total down to 532,000. This trend affected not only council-held sites. British Rail was finding its allotments more trouble than they were worth. In 1950 the company had 75,000 plots, but after this date they were disappearing at the rate of 3,000 a year. The loss of 8,000 kilometers/5,000 miles of railway in the 'Beeching Axe' of the 1960s did not help. Meanwhile, the National Coal Board, which had provided 7,000 plots through the war, let the leases expire.

**Poor image** — Allotments were getting a bad reputation. Scruffy huts made out of any old junk, and unkempt plots were all too common. Buying anything new was considered nouveau riche in allotment circles, a view still not appreciated by outsiders. Allotments in the North and the Midlands were used as much for pigeon-racing and keeping livestock as growing vegetables. The allotmenteer was caricatured as an old man in a cloth cap who escaped to his plot to get away from his missus. Professor Thorpe described him scathingly as 'an individualist who considers his allotment to be as private as his home garden, who is seldom interested in anything beyond its boundaries, and is blind to his further responsibilities'.

Councils, on the other hand, were blamed by plot holders and their supporters for giving allotments low priority. It was believed

that some councils failed to provide essential basic facilities – **Councils under fire**
water, fencing, and gates with locks to deter vandals – in order
to discourage and drive out plot holders. Having thus cleared
the site, they could claim that there was no demand and sell the land
to developers. By the 1980s there were only around 300,000 plots left
– a loss of more than 23,000 a year since 1970.

After the Thorpe Report, no further attempt was made to stem
this tragic downhill spiral, or find the causes for it, until 1997 – some
thirty years later. Inspired action came from an unexpected source.
The weekly *Amateur Gardening* magazine decided that it would step
into the breach. Having got backing from the NSALG, and with
high-profile soap stars Bill Treacher (Arthur in *EastEnders*) and
Thelma Barlow (Mavis in *Coronation Street*) as patrons, the
magazine launched its self-funded 'Allotments 2000' campaign **Allotments 2000 campaign**
in some style.

The main aim was to instigate a cross-party parliamentary
inquiry into the future of allotments in the UK, in order to raise their
profile and promote 'maximum use'. The campaigners hoped for a
reassessment of the number, location and usage of plots. They wanted
to press for more land dedicated to allotments and for there to be a
wider variation of how plots could be used, possibly for additional
leisure activities. A further vital issue on the agenda was to ensure
that existing allotment sites were fully protected from being sold off.

Following television appearances and a vigorous press campaign,
they succeeded in prevailing on the government. On 24 June 1998, a
parliamentary inquiry into the future of allotments was opened.
The Select Committee for the Environment, Transport and **Select committee investigates**
Regional Affairs concluded in its subsequent report that the
performance of local authorities was 'patchy', that 'while some
authorities pursue an active approach to maintaining vibrant and
fully-occupied allotment sites, others appear at best lethargic and
at worst to be instrumental in encouraging the decline of interest
in allotments.' Echoing the Thorpe Report, the select committee
proposed an urgent overhaul of allotment law, which it described as
'over prescriptive in some areas and under prescriptive in others'.

Furthermore, the legislation was 'very old' and 'spread over a dozen different statutes'.

The report recommended that decisions on the use of plots – with regard to flower-growing, commercial use, site shops, the sale of surplus produce and the keeping of livestock – should be made according to the needs of individual sites by the local authority or allotment society. Local authorities would be expected to provide water and fencing on all sites. They should encourage demand for allotments by advertising vacant plots in the local media and on information boards.

**Role of local authorities**

The inquiry pointed out that replacement sites had been provided for only two of the fifty-one statutory sites lost between May 1997 and April 1998. That 'given the inevitable and progressive loss of private and temporary allotment sites', such a low replacement rate was 'unacceptable'. To counteract this problem, temporary sites that had been in continuous use as allotments for at least thirty years should be given statutory status. For all other temporary sites, local authorities should indicate both the likely date for any change of use and the nature of that change.

**Replacement sites**

Any alternative allotment site offered 'should be of similar size and quality, within reasonable walking distance from existing plot holders' houses and should be given statutory protection'. Where no suitable replacement site was available, the report recommended that 'a significant proportion of the proceeds from the sale of the original site should be used to provide improvements to other allotment sites within the authority's area.'

## Growing in the community

The government's single action resulting from the parliamentary inquiry was to sponsor a guide to best practice, *Growing in the Community* (2001). This forward-looking handbook encouraged councils to promote allotments, and advocated that local authorities communicate with each other to foster a shared appreciation of how allotments could help deliver 'a diverse range of agendas, such as health, biodiversity and social inclusion'

**Best practice**

– a new and important perspective on allotments. The guide also proposed that councils allow plot holders to play a greater part in managing their own sites.

The Allotment Regeneration Initiative (ARI) was set up to spread the word. Funded by a charitable grant and headed by a steering group of experts, its main aim was to help councils put *Growing in the Community* into practice. Another important objective was to revive public interest in allotments, which were thought to be under 'considerable threat from neglect and development'. The ARI went on to produce its own *Good Sites Guide* (2004) and *Allotments: A Plotholders' Guide* (2007). It also supported the publication of *A Place to Grow* and the Scottish Allotment and Garden Society's *Allotments: A Scottish Plotholder's Guide* (2010).

To back its theories up with practical examples, the ARI helped turn around struggling allotments in Leicester by advertising on the back of buses and encouraging wildlife-friendly allotment management. It helped import tons of sand and manure to lighten the heavy clay at the neglected Chinbrook Manor Allotments in South London, bringing the place back to life and obtaining recognition for part of it as a 'site of borough importance for nature conservation'. The ARI ventured into Northern Ireland, where allotments are 'few and far between', and helped set up a pilot scheme there. The initiative's own 'Beers and Buses' travel bursary enabled groups to visit model allotments.

**ARI in action**

From 2009, the ARI ran a series of Allotment Officers' Forums across the country, for local authority employees to share their experiences. Volunteer mentors were made available to help plot holders, allotment associations, allotment officers, town and parish clerks and other groups keen to create new allotments. In 2012, however, the programme came to an end and ARI was absorbed into the NSALG.

## Green issues & an allotment renaissance

*Growing in the Community* sold well, and many of the ideas it contained were taken up by councils and plot holders alike. Dr Richard Wiltshire, one of the guide's authors and a senior lecturer at King's College, London, was to recall subsequently that the second edition, published in 2008, was 'set against a very different background'. 'Growing your own' had become fashionable, and there was no denying increasing levels of demand for allotments.

**Rising demand**

The world had woken up to green issues. This represented a major change of attitude, as chemicals had been actively encouraged in the 1947 Agriculture Act and had been liberally used by farmers and gardeners ever since. However, a few enlightened and far-sighted individuals questioned the wisdom of this approach. Lady Eve Balfour (1898–1990), niece of the prime minister Arthur Balfour, was one of the first women to study agriculture at Reading University. She went on to write a book about organic farming, *The Living Soil* (1943), and in 1946 founded the Soil Association in Suffolk, with a view to researching the effects of chemicals on the soil, crops, countryside and wildlife, as well as on the health of humans and livestock. Inspired by this example, in 1954 Lawrence Hills began the Henry Doubleday Research Association (now the national charity, Garden Organic) to test comfrey as a natural fertilizer and to promote organic growing. In 1962 a further wake-up call came from the American natural history writer, Rachel Carson, whose eloquent book the *Silent Spring* shocked a generation.

**Lady Eve Balfour & Lawrence Hills**

It took a few more generations for environmental issues to become of political importance. But in 1992 Britain and another 179 nations signed 'Agenda 21' at the Rio Earth Summit, to promote sustainability, or improve the quality of life while protecting the environment. This international commitment was reaffirmed in a document entitled 'The Future We Want' in 2012. Meanwhile, the British government introduced the Organic Aid Scheme to help farmers convert to organic growing over a period of two to five years. The Soil Association found its membership swelled dramatically as a result, as did public interest in organic farming. In addition to the current 4 per cent of organic farms in Britain, numerous other outlets are springing up – at farmers' markets, in independent shops and through 'vegetable box' schemes.

**Boost to organic farming**

While the BBC sitcom *The Good Life* inspired the first grow-your-own boom in the 1970s, there is no doubt that the more recent allotment surge has largely been due to concern for the environment. A desire to reduce 'food miles', problems such as BSE (mad cow disease) and fears over genetic engineering all played a part in reviving interest in home-grown food.

**New incentives to 'grow your own'**

The Food for Life Partnership was set up in 2006 to 'transform food culture' in schools – both growing and eating.

In addition, worries about poor nutrition and obesity have resulted in huge efforts to educate the young. Surprisingly, it was the catering manager of a primary school, Jeannette Orrey, who kicked off a food revolution which was to lead to school meals being put on the political agenda at national level. In 2000, at the height of the food scares, she decided to stop buying in school dinners for St Peter's Primary School in Nottinghamshire, and to cater for the children in-house using organic, local food. Her efforts came to the ears of celebrity chef Jamie Oliver, and inspired him to launch his high-profile schools campaign aimed at the 'lost generation' of children who 'don't know where their food comes from'.

In 2006, an even more ambitious project was formed in the Food for Life Partnership (FFLP) funded by a handsome National Lottery grant. The Soil Association, Garden Organic,

**Better food in schools**

the Focus on Food campaign and the Health Education Trust joined forces with the single aim of forming a countrywide network of schools and communities 'committed to transforming food culture'. Jeannette Orrey, now an MBE, is head of the nationwide School Cooks network and FFLP's school meals policy adviser, touring the country as ambassador.

**MBE**

The Royal Horticultural Society responded to growing public interest by setting up its campaign for school gardening, which since 2000 has gone into 15,000 schools and taught 3 million children about gardening. This was followed by 'Get Your Grown-ups Growing', an imaginative way for children to spur on the adults. Garden Organic also set up a Master Gardener programme to train and send volunteers out into the community to encourage wider vegetable growing.

Increased interest in good health, local food and

Not so different from the Ministry of Food posters to teach people how to grow food all year in the Second World War, a Food for Life poster with the same message for school children.

organic growing has resulted in a twenty-first century renaissance of allotments. Allotment fervour even reached the White House, where Michelle Obama converted part of the lawn into an extravagant vegetable plot. A kitchen garden was also installed

**White House vegetables**

(somewhat briefly) at Buckingham Palace for the first time since the Second World War.

People are clamouring to grow their own produce. In Britain there are still 300,000 council plots (just as there were in 1980), but the number of people on waiting lists, according to the NSALG, is now in the region of 90,000. The private sector has certainly risen to the occasion. British Waterways, the Crown Estate, the Church, railway companies and the National Trust have all provided land for plots. Landshare, launched in 2009, has also helped fill the gap by putting thousands of people who want to grow together with people who have land to spare.

**Landshare**

The growing bonanza of the 1990s has led to 'guerilla' gardening, New York style, in the cities and even concreted areas being turned into vibrant growing spaces with vegetables overflowing in builders' bags.

Brownfield and inner-city building sites awaiting finance have been turned over for temporary growing spaces as part of this wildly fashionable growing bonanza. Vacant expanses of concrete have been made into vibrant growing spaces filled with groups of builders' bags and palettes. 'Guerilla gardening', New York-style, has cropped up in unused corners of towns and cities. In Todmorden, West Yorkshire, and now in Conwy, Wales, Incredible Edible has turned every bit of bare earth into an opportunity for growing

**Incredible Edible**

National Allotments Week in August each year, under the NSALG umbrella,
runs countrywide competitions with a team of travelling judges.

vegetables. The annual Edible Garden Show held at Alexandra Palace, London, was launched in response to the 'grow-your-own revolution'. The NSALG's National Allotments Week, which takes place every August, includes countrywide competitions run by travelling judges.

## What of the future?

Despite all the enthusiasm, it seems unlikely that we will get more statutory allotments from the councils. Allan Rees, NSALG's chairman, deplores as a clever dodge the fact that councils are creating community gardens, since these have no legal protection against closure, unlike statutory allotments. The Federation of City Farms and Community Gardens, set up in 1980, has broadened its remit. Its new offshoot, the Community Land Advisory Trust, promotes community gardening and farming in all forms and brokers land access agreements.

**Community gardens**

The problem, of course, is largely one of space and priorities in a heavily populated country. Local government must choose between allotments – which make no money – and the needs for housing, transport, industry and business, which do, and are regarded by many as more important. The greatest fear for the safety of allotments is that the old laws securing them could be repealed at a stroke should the need arise. In 1979, and again in 2012, the government issued a White Paper proposing to repeal one of the crucial clauses that protect statutory allotments from being sold off too easily. This is Section 8 of the 1925 Allotment Act, which states that statutory allotments cannot be closed without the agreement of the secretary of state.

**Facing reality**

The NSALG put up a fierce fight and, backed by hefty pressure from the public, managed to force a retreat on both occasions. Had the act been repealed, the society later commented, it would have been 'devastating to the whole allotment movement'. Without the ministerial check, any local authority seeking to take over statutory allotment land for other purposes would become 'prosecutor, judge and jury in its own cause'.

**NSALG as watchdog**

Many argue that we may need allotments to feed the nation, as we did in wartime, if global warming and population growth cause food shortages. Marguerite Patten, the Second World War nutritionist, has expressed the widely held view that we have another war on, this time 'fighting recession rather than Hitler'. The NSALG notes that when times are hard, people 'turn back to the land'.

**A gift worth defending**

Above all, we need allotments for the great benefits they bring to physical and mental health, community spirit, integration and companionship (or, conversely, solitude and peace in a hectic world). Allotments are oases for people, providing a creative outlet, and havens for wildlife.

The long and bitter history of the fight for land provides a further reason to not let allotments slip away. They were hard-won but so easily could be lost. One group that honours the struggle it took to win them is the land-rights campaign, The Land is Ours. George Monbiot, the group's founder and a *Guardian* newspaper columnist, points out that while only 4 per cent of land in England and Wales is still registered as commons, the public have the right to roam on only a meagre one-fifth of this 'fragmentary inheritance'.

**The Land is Ours**

In 1999, 'a ragged band' of The Land is Ours activists marched to St George's Hill in Surrey and laid a plaque on the very spot where Gerrard Winstanley and the True Levellers had set up camp and started growing vegetables 350 years before. They also celebrated the 450th anniversary of Kett's Rebellion, the causes of which they link to today's issues of homelessness and public access to land. On this occasion, their destination was Mousehold Heath, north of Norwich. There they planted a tree to replace the lost 'oak of reformation', on the spot where the rebels held their councils of war, to honour Kett and the 2,650 Norfolk people who had died in protest against the enclosures and the loss of the ancient right for all of us to have a share in the common land.

Nostalgic sign on an allotment greenhouse, harking back to the time when farmers and gardeners pulled together to feed the nation.

# EPILOGUE

For many, the greatest pleasure on the allotment is the camaraderie, but my delight is having it selfishly all to myself. The early morning, when the only company is the robin which hops around hopefully to see what I might unearth, and the odd frog that scuttles with remarkable speed into the undergrowth, is a magical time for me, one when I live entirely for the moment.

Allotments these days cater for many needs quite other than growing food. The last decade or so has seen them transformed from basic utilitarian spaces – still carrying the offensive whiff of poverty and charity – into a more recreational and inclusive resource for society as a whole.

Highly motivated committees are taking up the reins of management from the over-stretched council allotment officer to great effect. Unlike the poor allotmenteer of old who could be pushed around and hoodwinked, these committees have the education and skills to make a strong case should any danger loom. They seek out grants that will help them provide a service to the community. Efforts are increasingly being made to draw in the dispossessed and the isolated, and so put a little cheer into their lives.

Allotments are now seen as a vital resource for nature conservation in towns and cities, and more attention is being paid to their role as sanctuaries for wildlife. As a result of intensive farming, it is estimated that one million countryside ponds have been wiped out, and 90 per cent of wildflower meadows. The latest concern is the demise of the bee, essential to life on earth, and now predominantly found in private gardens and beehives on allotments.

A new trend these days is the change in attitude towards the long-established dictum about growing 'mostly vegetables'. Allotmenteers have always been individualists and now they have a freer reign for self-expression. Flowers abound. While visiting different sites I have come across a doctor raising sweet peas for his surgery, a showman whose plot is almost entirely populated with prize dahlias for the local flower show (or an international one), an artist who cultivates irises for flower painting, and a woman who grows material for her herbal workshops. Travelling around, you will also find vineyards, dovecotes, hen-houses, communal orchards, story-telling chairs and sensory gardens. The more enterprising sites run open days, festivals, classes, lectures, and cater for special groups.

It could be said that allotments are not just more fun but that they serve more purpose for the community and the environment than ever before. Yet, if a strip on the commons had not been a matter of life and death for the medieval serf we would not be enjoying them today. Having delved into the history, I, for one, will never see allotments again in quite the same light. Remembering the struggle it took over centuries to win them makes them even more precious. My hope is that you will agree.

> 'The time has come,' the Walrus said,
> 'To talk of many things:
> Of shoes—and ships—and sealing-wax—
> Of cabbages—and kings—
> And why the sea is boiling hot—
> And whether pigs have wings.'

from 'The Walrus and the Carpenter' by Lewis Carroll (1872)

# FURTHER READING

Archer, John E. *Social Unrest and Popular Protest in England 1780–1840.* Cambridge University Press 2000

Bennett, H.S. *Life on the English Manor: A Study of Peasant Conditions 1150-1400.* Cambridge University Press 1937

Brereton, Geoffrey (ed). *Froissart: Chronicles.* Penguin Books 1968

Buchan, Ursula. *A Green and Pleasant Land: How England's Gardeners Fought the Second World War.* Hutchinson 2013

Burchardt, Jeremy. *The Allotment Movement in England 1793–1873.* Boydell Press 2002

Burchardt, Jeremy & Cooper, Jacqueline (eds). *Breaking New Ground: Nineteenth Century Allotments from Local Sources.* FACHRS Publications 2010

Butcher, Gerald W. *Allotments for All: The Story of a Great Movement.* Allen & Unwin 1918

Cobbett, William. *Rural Rides.* Penguin Classics (1830) 2001

Crouch, David & Ward, Colin. *The Allotment: Its Landscape and Culture.* Faber and Faber 1988

Dunn, Alastair. *The Peasants' Revolt: England's Failed Revolution of 1381.* Tempus 2002

Eden, Sir Frederick Morton. *The State of the Poor: An History of the Labouring Classes in England, from the Conquest to the Present Period.* Cambridge University Press 2011

Fearnley-Whittingstall, Jane. *The Ministry of Food: Thrifty Wartime Ways to Feed Your Family Today.* Hodder & Stoughton 2010

George, M. Dorothy. *London Life in the Eighteenth Century.* Kegan Paul, Trench, Trubner 1925

Green, F. E. *A History of the English Agricultural Labourer 1870–1920.* Forgotten Books 2012

Gregory, Adrian. *The Last Great War: British Society and the First World War.* Cambridge University Press 2008

Hammond, J.L. & Barbara. *The Village Labourer 1760–1832: A Study in the Government of England Before the Reform Bill.* Longman 1978

Hanawalt, Barbara A. *The Ties that Bound: Peasant Families in Medieval England.* Oxford University Press 1986

Hasbach, Wilhelm. *A History of the English Agricultural Labourer.* P.S. King & Son 1908

Hilton, Rodney. *Bond Men Made Free.* Routledge (1973) 2003

Hoskins, W.G. *The Making of the English Landscape.* Hodder & Stoughton 1955

Kenyon, John. *The Civil Wars of England.* Weidenfeld & Nicolson 1988

Marsh, Jan. *Back to the Land: The Pastoral Impulse in Victorian England from 1880 to 1914.* Quartet Books 1982

Mathias, Peter. *The First Industrial Nation: An Economic History of Britain 1700–1914.* Methuen 1969

Middleton, C.H. *Digging for Victory: Wartime Gardening with Mr. Middleton.* Aurum Press 2008

Mingay, G.E. *Parliamentary Enclosure in England: An Introduction to its Causes, Incidence and Impact 1750–1850.* Addison Wesley Longman 1997

Mingay, G.E. (ed). *The Victorian Countryside.* Routledge & Keegan Paul 1981

Minns, Raynes. *Bombers and Mash: The Domestic Front 1939–45.* Virago Press 1999

Neeson, J.M. *Commoners: Common Right, Enclosure and Social Change in England 1700–1820.* Cambridge University Press 1993

Neilson, Nellie. *Customary Rents.* Forgotten Books (1910) 2012

O'Brien, Mark. *When Adam Delved and Eve Span: A History of the Peasants' Revolt of 1381.* New Clarion Press 2004

Oman, Charles William Chadwick. *The Great Revolt of 1381.* Forgotten Books (1906) 2012.

Overton, Mark. *Agricultural Revolution in England: The Transformation of the Agrarian Economy 1500-1850.* Cambridge University Press 1995

Patten, Marguerite. *Victory Cookbook: Nostalgic Food and Facts from 1940–1954.* Chancellor Press 2002

Poole, Steve. *The Allotment Chronicles: A Social History of Allotment Gardening.* Silver Link 2006

Power, Eileen. *Medieval People.* Methuen 1950

Smith, Daniel. *The Spade as Mighty as the Sword: The Story of World War Two's Dig for Victory Campaign.* Aurum Press 2011

Snell, K.D.M. *Annals of the Labouring Poor: Social Change and Agrarian England 1660–1900.* Cambridge University Press 1985

Ward, Colin. *Cotters and Squatters: Housing's Hidden History.* Five Leaves 2002

Wilson, A.N. *The Victorians.* Hutchinson 2002

Wiltshire, Richard & Burn, Deborah. *Growing in the Community.* Local Government Association 2008

Wood, Andy. *Riot, Rebellion and Popular Politics in Early Modern England.* Palgrave 2002

Ziegler, Philip. *The Black Death.* History Press (1969) 2010

# TIMELINE

The main events – wars, famines, uprisings, enquiries, movements, initiatives and laws – covered in the book are listed here for reference.
The four allotment acts still on the statute book (1908, 1922, 1925 and 1950) are marked with an asterisk*.

**1066 Battle of Hastings** brings defeat for King Harold, leading to the Norman Conquest of England.

**1086 Domesday Book** is made by order of William I to record land ownership.

**1215 Magna Carta** is signed by King John.

**1235 Statute of Merton** allows an owner to 'inclose' common land where there is an excess of it beyond the commoners' needs.

**1315–1317 Great Famine** results from cold, rainy summers.

**1327–1377 Reign of Edward III** sees the evolution of Parliament.
The Commons (knights, burgesses and citizens) and Lords (barons and clergy) deliberate separately.

**1337 Edward III** lays claim to the French throne and the Hundred Years War begins.

**1348 Black Death** reaches Britain.

**1349 Ordinance of Labourers** caps the wages that can be paid to labourers. This is endorsed by the **1351 Statute of Labourers**.

**1358 Jacquerie** in northern France, in which peasants rise up against the nobles.

**1377 First Poll Tax.** France invades England. Richard II becomes king.

**1379 Second Poll Tax.** John of Gaunt leads an unsuccessful assault on France.

**1380 Third Poll Tax.** Archbishop Sudbury is appointed chancellor, and Sir Robert Hales becomes treasurer. A further invasion of France is planned.

**1381 Peasants' Revolt** led by Wat Tyler, John Ball and Jack Straw.

**1453 Hundred Years War** ends.

**1489 Law to deter enclosure** is passed. Half of any profit from land where houses are pulled down must go to the Crown until the houses are rebuilt.

**1495 Vagabonds and Beggars Act** stipulates that 'idle and suspected' persons are to be sent to the stocks for three days and nights on bread and water before being expelled.

**1515 Conversion from arable to pasture** becomes an offence.

**1517 Cardinal Wolsey** launches a national enquiry into illegal enclosures.

**1533 Law to restrict sheep farming** is put in place.

**1534 Act of Supremacy**, by which Henry VIII breaks from the Roman Catholic Church.

**1536 Dissolution of the monasteries** begins in England and Wales.

**1548 Enquiry commissioned under Edward VI** into which towns, villages and hamlets have been 'decayed and laid down by enclosures into pastures'.

**1549 Kett's Rebellion** takes place in Norfolk.

**1562 Statute of Artificers**, passed during Elizabeth I's reign, requires a seven-year apprenticeship for skilled artisans.

**1563 Tillage Act** for the 'maintenance of husbandry and tillage', aims to prevent the conversion of arable to pasture and subsequent depopulation.

**1589 Planning Act against Erecting and Maintaining Cottages.** New cottages are to have four acres (1.6 hectares) attached to provide some self-sufficiency. This is the first appearance of the idea of providing land to counteract poverty.

**1601 Elizabethan Poor Law.** Parishes become responsible for their own poor, administered by Justices of the Peace and overseers.

**1607 Midland Revolt** led by Captain Pouch.

**1642 English Civil War** begins.

**1645 Cromwell's New Model Army** is formed.

**1649 Gerrard Winstanley and the True Levellers** take over St George's Hill, Surrey.

**1649 English Civil War** ends. Charles I is executed.

**1656 Last anti-enclosure bill** is rejected.

**1660 Restoration** of Charles II

**1662 Settlement and Removal Act** establishes the need to prove 'settlement' before applying for poor relief. Corporation workhouses are introduced.

**1697 Badging the poor.** Paupers on poor relief are to wear a coloured cloth on the right shoulder, bearing the letter 'P' and the initial of the parish. This regulation is not abolished until 1810.

**1715 Riot Act** gives the army *carte blanche* to deal with rioters that do not disperse when the act is read out.

**1723 Knatchbull's Act** introduces the 'workhouse test'. Those applying for poor relief have to enter the workhouse and carry out work in return for the parish's help.

**1750s Parliamentary enclosures increase** in number. This is the process by which landowners petition Parliament to secure private acts of enclosure.

**1782 Gilbert's Act** restricts workhouses to the old, sick and orphans. The able-bodied are to be found work on a subsistence wage. **Parliamentary act** allows up to 10 acres (4 hectares) of waste land adjacent to the workhouse to be enclosed by the Guardians of the Poor, in order to assist those on parish relief. This is extended in 1801, permitting small plots to be joined up and worked in common.

**1784 Threshing machine** is invented by Andrew Meikle.

**1792 French Revolutionary Wars** begin.

**1795 Speenhamland System** tops up wages according to the price of bread.

**1796 Society for Bettering the Condition and Increasing the Comforts of the Poor** is founded.

**1801 Enclosure Consolidation Act** provides a common framework to streamline the process of enclosure by private act of parliament.

**1802 Launch of the** *Political Register*, William Cobbett's revolutionary newspaper.

**1809 Allotments of Great Somerford, Wiltshire**, are established – can be seen as possibly the first ever allotment site.

**1811–1816 Luddites** protest against mechanization.

**1815 Napoleonic Wars** end.

**1819 Peterloo massacre**, in which the cavalry attacks crowds gathered for a political rally at St Peter's Field, Manchester.

**1830 Swing Riots** rage across southern Britain.

**1831 Labourers' Friend Society** is founded by Benjamin Wills. It promotes self-help and provides landowners with advice on setting up allotments.

**1832 Great Reform Act.** One in six males are enfranchised.

**1832–1834 Poor Law Commissioners' Report**

**1833 Abolition of Slavery**

**1834 Poor Law Amendment Act** brings an end to outdoor relief. The only help for the poor is now the workhouse. Union workhouses are introduced.

**1834 Tolpuddle martyrs**, who tried to form a secret trade union, are sentenced to transportation.

**1836 Enclosure Act.** It is no longer necessary for landowners to go to Parliament to secure an enclosure, as long as there is a majority agreement among the interested parties.

**1838–1848 Chartists** campaign for parliamentary reform, including universal suffrage for men.

**1843 Select Committee on the Labouring Poor (Allotments of Land)** recommends, for example, that plots should be provided close to the labourer's dwelling.

**1845 General Enclosure Act** includes the requirement that Charity Commissioners provide the landless poor with 'field gardens' no larger than one-quarter of an acre (0.1 hectares). **Potato blight strikes Britain**, first in the Isle of Wight. **Great Irish Famine** begins.

**1846 Repeal of the Corn Laws** under Robert Peel results in cheap corn being imported from America.

**1867 Second Reform Act** doubles the suffrage to two out of five males, with a property qualification.

**1868 Trades Union Congress** is founded.

**1873 First official census of allotments** covers the number of plots in rural areas, but not in the towns, where they are becoming significant.

**1872 National Agricultural Labourers' Union** is founded by Joseph Arch.

**1882 Allotments Extension Act** is proposed by MP Jesse Collings. Poor Law Commissioners and charity trustees could be forced by the Charity Commissioners to let out land allocated to the poor as allotments.

**1884 Third Reform Act** extends the vote, enfranchising 60 per cent of adult males and giving the counties the same franchise as the boroughs.

**1886 Salisbury government is brought down** when Jesse Collings calls for an amendment to the Queen's Speech.

**1887 Allotments Act.** Local sanitary authorities are obliged to provide allotments if any six registered local voters request them and where there is no provision. The limit is set at one acre (0.4 hectares) per plot.

**1889 Board of Agriculture** incorporates all government departments dealing with different aspects of agriculture.

**1890 Allotment Act** makes it mandatory for county councils to have a standing committee on allotments, which can hold inquiries into failures by the sanitary authorities to get land for plots.

**1901 Agricultural Organization Society**, a member cooperative, is founded to give advice and assistance to 'properly registered cooperative societies'. It later becomes the Allotment Organization Society.

**1906–1914 Liberal welfare reforms** include the introduction of old age pensions, free school meals, National Insurance and labour exchanges.

**1907 Small Holdings and Allotments Act** imposes a duty on urban, borough and parish councils to provide allotments where there is a demand.

**1908\* Small Holdings and Allotments Act** is the basis of modern allotment law. It endorses the 1887, 1890 and 1907 acts and imposes further responsibilities on councils. They are empowered to make compulsory purchases of allotments, and also to sell them if they are 'of the opinion' that they are no longer needed. Local authorities must provide sufficient allotments, according to demand. Also in 1908, **National Farmers' Union** is founded.

**1914 First World War** begins. **Defence of the Realm Act (DORA)** comes into force, giving the government wide-ranging powers – including the right to commandeer resources for the war effort.

**1916 Cultivation of Lands Order** means that local authorities can requisition vacant urban land for food-growing for the duration of the war.

**1917 Germany declares unrestricted submarine warfare** and targets merchant ships carrying Britain's food supply. **Women's Land Army** starts up.

**1917 National Union of Allotment Holders** is established from many small societies. Links are forged with the Cooperative Unions and the Distributive Union of Cooperative Stores, which provide gardening goods at trade prices and an outlet for the sale of surplus produce.

**1918 First World War** ends. **Representation of the People Act** enfranchises all men over twenty-one and women over thirty.

**1919 Land Settlement (Facilities) Act** makes more land available to help returning servicemen. Smallholders can buy land on credit and pay it back over sixty years. This act makes allotments open to all, not only the 'labouring population'.

**1919 'Addison' or Housing and Town Planning Act** aims for 5 million 'homes fit for heroes'.

**1922\* Allotments Act** limits plots to a quarter of an acre (0.1 hectares). Establishes a six-month period of notice (three months where the land is urgently needed for building) and increases compensation. Councils are required to set up allotment committees. The act defines allotments as 'an area not exceeding forty poles which is wholly or mainly cultivated by the occupier for the production of vegetable crops for consumption by himself and his family'.

**1925\* Allotments Act** requires authorities to take into account the need for allotments in town planning. Any ground purchased by a local authority for allotments is statutory and cannot be converted to other use without ministerial permission.

**1926 General Strike.** The Quaker **Society of Friends** helps unemployed miners through its Coalfields Distress Committee and, from the 1930s, its Allotment Committee.

**1927 Trades Disputes Act** bans sympathy strikes and mass picketing.

**1928 Representation of the People Act** extends the voting franchise to all women over the age of twenty-one.

**1929 Local Government Act** abolishes all Poor Law Unions and replaces them by 'public assistance'.

**1929 Wall Street Crash**

**1930 National Allotments Society** founded incorporating the Allotments Organization Society, Small Holders Ltd. and the National Union of Allotment Holders.

**1939 Second World War** begins.

**1939 Cultivation of Lands Order** enables councils to seize land, as in the First World War. Other emergency regulations affecting land use come into effect. **Defence Regulation 61** makes trespass on allotments a statutory offence. **Defence Regulation 62A** allows local councils to requisition unoccupied land for allotments and to use parks and playing fields for vegetable growing. **Defence Regulation 62B** permits livestock on allotments.

**1940 Dig for Victory campaign** is underway. **Rationing** is brought in.

**1942 Beveridge Report** recommends a national welfare system.

**1945 Second World War** ends.

**1946 National Insurance Act.** Lady Eve Balfour founds the **Soil Association**.

**1948 National Assistance Act** repeals the Poor Law of 1834.

**1948 Repeal of the Settlement Act of 1662** (which said that poor relief was only available in parish of origin).

**1948 Representation of the People Act** brings in one person one vote. Extends the suffrage to local elections (apart from Northern Ireland, which has to wait until 1968).

**1950\* Allotment Act** extends the notice to quit to twelve months. Permits the keeping of bees and poultry on allotments.

**1952 Rationing** ends.

**1965 Thorpe Committee** is set up to review policy on allotments.

**1998 Parliamentary Inquiry into the Future of Allotments** makes recommendations on management and good practice, published as *Growing in the Community* (2001 & 2008). **Allotment Regeneration Initiative** is established and runs forums for allotment officers.

**2005 National Allotment Week** becomes an annual fixture.

**2008 Incredible Edible**, a community gardening scheme, comes into being in Todmorden, West Yorkshire.

**2009 Landshare** created, to put growers looking for land in touch with people with land to spare. One of its aims is to free up land for growing.

# INDEX

Page numbers in *italics* refer to captions

# ACKNOWLEDGMENTS

My sincerest thanks to Helen Griffin, Editorial Director of Gardens and Gardening at Frances Lincoln, for a highly enjoyable collaboration, and to Sarah Higgens who precision-edited my text with unfailing patience and considerable panache. Heartfelt thanks go also to my wise friends who read the manuscript and came up with invaluable advice – publisher Rosemary Wilkinson, journalist Pearson Phillips, historian Tony Neville and my harshest critic but lifelong friend, Bill Scobie.

# PICTURE CREDITS

Front cover image: 'Dig for Plenty. Grow food in your garden or get an allotment'. 1939–45. This is a reworking of a 'Dig For Victory' poster, presumably for use after the end of the war. National Archives. Wikimedia Commons.

7 Drovers with a Pair of Rearing Horses by Thomas Rowlandson 1756–1827. Joseph F. McCrindle Collection. National Gallery of Art.

9 Two Peasants Drinking by Adriaen van Ostade (1610–85). Joseph F. McCrindle Collection. National Gallery of Art.

15 King William I. (The Conqueror). Artist unknown. National Portrait Gallery. Wikimedia Commons.

17 Historical brewing sign from the Housebook of the Mendel Family 1437.

18 'September: harvesting, ploughing and sowing', from a Book of Hours, c.1540. The Bridgeman Art Library. Getty Images.

21 'Peasants Lunching in the Open Air' by Esias van de Velde (1590–1630). Rosemwald Collection. National Gallery of Art.

25 'Old Woman'. Watercolour by Thomas Rowlandson (1756–1827). Joseph F. McCrindle Collection. National Gallery of Art.

29 'Medieval Black Death'. © Roberto Castillo. Shutterstock.

30 Black Death. Miniature from the Toggenburg Bible (Switzerland). 1411. Wikimedia Commons.

31 Plague doctors. Costume d'un Medecin de Lazaret de Marseille en 1720 Wellcome Library, London.

34 Richard II, unknown artist. C. 1390. Westminster Abbey. Wikimedia Commons.

36 'Man in Pillory' published L'Illustration, Journal Universel, Paris, 1860. © Antonio Abrignani. Shutterstock.

37 Detail of a miniature of the English landing in Normandy. Chroniques de France ou de St Denis (from 1270–1380). Last quarter of the 14th century, after 1380. Virgil Master and his atelier. Wikimedia Commons.

41 Peasant's Revolt. Manuscript copy of the Chronicles of Jean Froissart (c.1483). British Library. Wikimedia Commons.

42 Tower of London from a 15th century manuscript. A manuscript (British Library, MS Royal, 16 folio 73) of poems by Charles, Duke of Orléans (1391–1465). Wikimedia Commons.

44 Manuscript copy of the Chronicles of Jean Froissart (c.1483). Wikimedia Commons.

47 Detail from Sheep in pen being milked; women walking away bearing vessels, from the 'Luttrell Psalter', c.1325–35 (vellum), English School, (14th century)/British Library, London, UK/© British Library Board. All Rights Reserved/The Bridgeman Art Library.

49 Alphonse Legros (1837–1911). Farm at the Monastery. Rosemwald Collection. National Gallery of Art.

50–51 Ms 340/603 f.93 Calendar: 12 Scenes of the Labours of the Year, from 'Le Rustican' by Pietro de Crescenzi (1230–1320/1) c.1460 (vellum) (see 155574), French School, (15th century)/ Musée Conde, Chantilly, France/Giraudon/The Bridgeman Art Library.

55 Gustave Doré (1832–1883). Gypsy Children. Joseph F. McCrindle Collection. National Gallery of Art.

56 Jean-Baptiste-Camille Corot (1796–1875). Gypsy Girl with Mandolin. Gift of Count Cecil Pecci-Blunt. National Gallery of Art.

57 George Cuitt the Younger (1778–1854). Welsh Hovel at Machynlleaeth. Gift of John Nichols & Dorothy Coogan Estabrook. National Gallery of Art.

60 English: Execution of Hugh the Younger Despenser, from a manuscript of Froissart (Bibliotheque Nationale) 1470s. Wikimedia Commons.

63 Brienz fair, Berne. Created by Girardet, published on Magasin Pittoresque, Paris, 1850. Shutterstock.

64 Medieval bourgeois and craftsman, old engraved portrait. Created by Willemin, published on Magasin Pittoresque, Paris, 1844. Shutterstock.

68 The Rebellion under Kett the Tanner in the Oak of Reformation near Norwich. British Library/ Robana. Getty Images.

72 E: General Thomas Fairfax (1612–1671) by Robert Walker and Studio. Sothebys. Wikimedia Commons.

76 Robert Bakewell. F. Engleheart, sc.; published by Joseph Rogerson, 1849. Wikimedia Commons.

77 'Thomas William Coke MP for Norfolk inspecting sheep' by Thomas Weaver (1774–1843) from Gunby Hall, Lincolnshire. ©National Trust Images/John Hammond.

78 ' A Man Threshing Beside a Wagon, Farm Buildings behind' by Peter Paul Rubens. 1615–1617. Paul Getty Trust.

81 'Old engraved illustration of Threshing Machine or Thrashing Machine in the Field'. Industrial Encyclopedia E.O. Lam. 1875. Shutterstock.

83 'The Leader of the Parisian Blood Red Republic or the Infernal Fiend' by George Cruikshank. First published by the artist and sold by William Tweedie, London, June 1871. From the Graphic Works of George Cruikshank, by Richard A. Vogler. Dover Pictorial Archives, 1979.

87 Pieter Brueghel the Younger. 'The Payment of the Tithes'. 1626. Christies. Wikimedia Commons.

89 Map of distribution of enclosures 1750–1850 by the author after Parliamentary Enclosures of the Commons by E.C.K. Gonner.

91 'An Excrescence – a Fungus; alias – a Toadstool upon a Dunghill'. Caricature of William Pitt the Younger, published by Humphrey, London, 1971. From the Graphic Works of George Cruikshank, by Richard A. Vogler. Dover Pictorial Archives, 1979.

92 David Teniers the Younger (1610–1690). 'Two Peasants with a Glass of Wine'. Gift of Nell V. Weidenhammer. National Gallery of Art.

93 David Teniers the Younger (1610–1690). 'Peasants in a Tavern'. Gift of Mr. & Mrs. John Ely Pflieger on the 50th Anniversary of the National Gallery of Art.

101 'Posting to the election – a scene on the road to Brentford, November 1806'. James Gillray (1756–1815), National Portrait Gallery.

107 Captain Swing, Dedicated to Messrs Cobbett Carlisle and Co. British Museum. Below the title: 'taken from the Life. Dedicated to Messrs Cobbett, Carlisle, & Co'. A knock-kneed ruffian, with a sinister scowl, stands full-face with arms crossed on his chest; he holds a bludgeon, a letter addressed to To . . . Esq',... Published by S W Fores. Print: Henry Heath. 1830. British Museum.

108 Robert Peel (1788–1850). Engraved by J. Cochran and published in The Letters of Queen Victoria 1844–1853, United Kingdom, 1907. Shutterstock.

111 Arthur Wellesley, 1st Duke of Wellington (1769–1852). Engraved by H. Robinson and published in Fisher's Drawing Room Scrap Book, United Kingdom, 1837. Shutterstock.

119 'Peasant Couple with Cow' by Jacques Callot (1592–1635). R. L. Blaumfeld Collection. National Gallery of Art.

120 'Evicted family'. Irish potato famine 1840s. Photo by Universal History Archive/UIG via Getty Images.

122 Joseph Arch from the Canadian Illustrated News the 1869–1883. Wikimedia Commons.

123 'The Dorchester Unionists Imploring Merci (!!!) of their King'. Tolpuddle Martyrs, 1834. National Archives.

127 'Country man and woman' from 'La petite soeur par Hector Malot' (1882). © Hans Nouwens. Shutterstock.

129 'Dwellings of the poor in Bethnal Green, the state of the water supply'. Illustrated Times, 1863. Wellcome Library, London.

130 William Heath 'A Monster Soup commonly called Thames Water', 1828 Wellcome Library, London.

131 'A man well–prepared for the 1832 cholera epidemic in Nuremberg', c1832. Wellcome Library, London.

133 The Leader of the Luddites. 1812. Published by Messrs Walker and Knight, Royal Exchange. Artist unknown. Wikimedia Commons.

135 'Oliver Asking for More' by George Cruikshank first published in the first instalment of 'Oliver Twist or the Parish Boy's Progress' by Charles Dickens, 1837 in Bentley's Miscellany. From the Graphic Works of George Cruikshank, by Richard A. Vogler. Dover Pictorial Archives, 1979.

154 'Cornish prize-winner for harrowing, driving, and costume'. Photo from Great War magazine, vol. 156, UK, circa 1917. © Igor Goloniov. Shutterstock.

161 Postcard of man with onions on allotment 1917. Garden Museum.

164 The Cabinet Papers. General Strike. 1926 The Lever Breaks by Bernard Partridge. National Archive.

165 Winston Churchill by 'Matt' 1929 as illustrative material for a book on 'Contemporary Personalities' by the Earl of Birkenhead. Wikimedia Commons.

166 Miners Returning to Work at Newdigate Colliery 1926. Corbis Images.

169 Garden City Concept, originally published in 'Garden Cities of tomorrow' by Ebenezer Howard, Sonnenschein publishing, 1902. Wikimedia Commons.

175 Harvesting by Adrian Allinson. 1939–45. HMSO. Wikimedia Commons.

177 'Dig for Victory Says the Minister of Agriculture'. Leaflet: 'Grow More Food – Dig for Victory'. MAF 1939. Garden Museum.

179 Poster 'This Plan Will Give You Vegetables All Year Round'. Garden Museum.

180 Four-fold leaflet No.1 'Vegetable production in private gardens and allotments'. Introductory note from R.S. Hudson, cropping plan, storage, soil, potato blight. Issued by Ministry of Agriculture and Fisheries, 1941.

181 Wartime gardening books. © Francesca Foley.

186 'Up Housewives and at 'em…'. Artist Yates Wilson 1939–45. Collection of the National Archives (UK). Wikimedia Commons.

188 'Victory Gardens. Where the Nazi's sowed death, a Londoner and his wife have sown life-giving vegetables in a London Bomb crater'. Official British photo. 1943. National Archives. Wikimedia Commons.

192 Members of the British Women's Land Army harvesting beets. British Ministry of Information, from Fox Photos, c. 1943. Wikimedia Commons.

195 Harry Thorpe. Photo: University of Birmingham. Wikimedia Commons.

201 Seed Saving in Schools. Courtesy of Garden Organic and Food for life.

202 Food Growing Year. Courtesy of Food for Life.

203 Builders' Bags © Francesca Foley.

204 National Allotments Week 2012. Courtesy of the artist, Chris Cyprus and NSALG.

207 Photo shed and poster © Francesca Foley.